Number

Number

Activities for children with mathematical learning difficulties

Mel Lever

David Fulton Publishers
London

David Fulton Publishers Ltd
The Chiswick Centre, 414 Chiswick High Road, London W4 5TF

www.fultonpublishers.co.uk

David Fulton Publishers is a division of Granada Learning Limited, part of the Granada Media Group.

First published in 2003

10 9 8 7 6 5 4 3 2 1

Copyright © Mel Lever 2003

The right of Mel Lever to be identified as the author of this work has been asserted by her in accordance with the Copyright, Designs and Patents Act 1988.

British Library Cataloguing in Publication Data
A catalogue record for this book is available from the British Library.

ISBN 1-84346-948-3

The materials in this publication may be photocopied only for use in the purchasing organisation. Otherwise, all rights are reserved. No part of this publication may be reproduced, stored in a retrieval system or transmitted, in any form, or by any means, electronic, mechanical, photocopying, recording or otherwise, without the prior permission of the publishers.

Designed and typeset by Kenneth Burnley, Wirral, Cheshire
Cover design by Phil Barker
Printed and bound in Great Britain by Thanet Press Limited, Margate, Kent

Contents

	Foreword	vi
	Introduction to the Series	vii
	Acknowledgements	x
1	Number: Introduction	1
2	Memory Training	2
3	Numbers as Digits (1)	7
4	Numbers as Digits (2)	9
5	Number Bonds and Beach Huts	10
6	Teaching Number Bonds by Wearing Silly Hats	12
7	Number Bonds with an Addition Square	15
8	Number Bonds with a Difference Square	17
9	Place Value with Early Learners	19
10	Bonds and Loops	23
11	Place Value: The Mushroom Story	25
12	Place Value: Column Addition	28
13	Place Value: Standard Algorithm	29
14	Place Value: Column Subtraction	30
15	Place Value: Whole Numbers and Decimals	31
16	Missing Number Calculations	34
17	Bingo	36
18	The 100 Square	41
19	Fractions	47
20	Negative Numbers	52
21	What is the Bank Balance?	55
22	Mental Arithmetic	56
23	Mental Arithmetic Using Number Cards	58
24	Activities Using Dice	60
25	Practising Basic Number Skills with Monster Maths	63
26	Blockbusters	68
27	A Project on Travel	71
28	Who Wants to be a Maths Millionaire?	74
29	Multiplication Tables	77
30	Finger Tables	82
31	Three in a Row – a Tables Game	85

Foreword

Mel Lever is an inspirational teacher of mathematics because she can teach maths to children who don't understand it and don't like it. She contrasts with other gifted maths teachers who can teach maths to children who are good at it. Since there seem to be more pupils who find maths challenging, Mel's ability to break concepts down and to find a creative way of making them accessible is of huge importance.

Mel teaches at Fairley House School, a specialist school for pupils with specific learning difficulties. She teaches maths on a daily basis and, as Maths and Key Stage 2 Coordinator, offers advice and ideas to colleagues. She is also someone who continues to learn and is always ready to take on board new ideas offered by others. She gives workshops to parents on helping children to overcome mathematical difficulties and is in great demand on the lecture circuit for teachers. This set of books means that a wider audience of parents and teachers can be inspired by her ideas.

Mel has studied the teaching of maths for many years and is very familiar with research in the area, particularly into mathematical difficulties. However, she has always chosen to go beyond the theory and to address the vital question: 'So what shall we do about it?' This is what makes her books so helpful; they give parents and teachers practical ideas they can use. Mel addresses the question of the types of difficulty encountered, then moves on to overcoming the difficulty.

At a recent maths workshop for governors, a governor commented, 'I wish Mel had taught me maths when I was at school'. I can only echo that sentiment and urge the reader of these books to enjoy learning from Mel how to teach maths to children who struggle and lag behind.

Jackie Murray
Principal and Educational Psychologist
Fairley House School

Introduction to the Series

Introduction

There are many children who, despite dedicated teachers, the introduction of the National Numeracy Strategy, wonderful books, and an abundance of maths equipment, still do not enjoy or understand mathematics.

We should focus on the two words 'enjoy' and 'understand' because I feel that unless children enjoy their maths, they are unlikely to fully understand it. Children may appear to be functioning reasonably and be achieving set goals, but I am sure that many children could achieve more if they had a 'fun time' with their maths.

I teach dyslexic and dyspraxic children at Fairley House School in London, many of whom have difficulties in understanding maths concepts and functioning mathematically. Over the years I have had to develop ways of interesting these children and helping them to learn. I have diagnosed their difficulties and set about changing my teaching, and that of others, so that maths could be presented to the children in a meaningful and fun way.

It is worth looking at the field of dyslexia in order to summarise the many ways in which children find learning difficult.

The British Dyslexia Association lists many factors that indicate dyslexia. I have picked out the following as being particularly relevant when trying to understand the mathematical learning difficulties of our children:

- Shows confusion between direction words, e.g. up/down, in/out.
- Has difficulty with sequence, e.g. coloured bead sequence, and, later, days of the week.
- Has inability to remember the label for known objects, e.g. 'table', 'chair'.
- Has difficulty learning nursery rhymes and rhyming words, e.g. 'cat', 'mat', 'sat'.
- Has particular difficulty with reading and spelling.
- Puts letters and figures the wrong way round.
- Has difficulty remembering tables, alphabet, formulae, etc.
- Still occasionally confuses 'b' and 'd' and words such as 'no/on'.
- Still needs to use fingers or marks on paper to make simple calculations.
- Has poor concentration.
- Has problems processing language at speed.
- Has difficulty telling left from right, order of days of the week, months of the year, etc.
- Has poor sense of direction.

Other relevant points could be added to this list. Many children with dyslexia have difficulty with left and right orientation. Many young dyslexic children need aids for doing any arithmetical computation. Some relinquish these aids at the same developmental stage as would the average child. However, the dyslexic and dyspraxic child may well need these aids for a longer time.

Difficulties in recalling multiplication tables are caused by short-term memory problems and by the inability to easily recognise sequences and patterns, thus removing props that help when memory fails. This leads to difficulties with working at speed to solve mathematical problems or when memorising, not only multiplication facts, but also addition, subtraction and division facts. It also leads to difficulties with telling the time, remembering the days of the week and months of the year.

I can hear many teachers and parents saying, 'My child has some of these problems, but he is not dyslexic. Why concentrate on dyslexia?' The simple answer is that I am not concentrating on dyslexia. I am hoping that, by outlining the above, I will give the reader an idea of the issues I am faced with in my work with dyslexic children. Many children have mathematical learning difficulties for a variety of reasons. Because I have worked with children who have difficulties in many areas of the curriculum and in all areas of mathematics, I have been forced to think of ways to overcome these difficulties. In doing so, I have found ways of interesting all children: the devices, games and methods I have developed have been of interest to children in general and their teachers.

Teachers of maths to children with mathematical learning difficulties are aware that every statement or teaching point needs to be rephrased and produced in a variety of ways, using concrete and pictorial methods, if the child is to make any sense of it. Asking a child to accept a mathematical fact and use it is not always helpful. The child may lack reference points and be unable to latch on to any signpost; he or she may lack any internal visual stimulus.

Teachers are constantly diagnosing the learning of their pupils; they learn how to adapt their teaching in the light of knowledge gained. Thus teachers are instruments of change in a school setting and thence in the wider world. Each teacher has a unique view of the wider educational community in which he or she is involved.

My teaching experience has led to a conviction that much mathematical learning is inhibited through children not being offered a wide enough mathematical vocabulary. This does not mean always *adding words* to the vocabulary; it might often mean *adding meaning* to the words already used by the children.

How the series is organised

The National Numeracy Strategy and Maths Schemes are mostly arranged in the expectation of an ordered, sequential and predictable path of learning. Teachers know that this is not how children learn. Maths is not a narrow subject; it is not just a series of truisms and facts. Maths is about discovery and logic; it is about pattern and shape; it is about order and chaos. Anyone reading that last sentence will have a different view of its meaning. We all have a different way of seeing and understanding the various aspects of mathematics. Some aspects of maths are easy for us to understand, some are not.

I considered arranging this series of books into year order: Years 1 to 6 or 7. I then realised that it is impossible to categorise need in this way. The activities I am suggesting are suitable for children in all these years. The principles concerned are adaptable. There is no lower or upper age limit to their usefulness and interest.

I decided to produce a series of books covering the various aspects of mathematics as followed in schools: number, shape and space, measures and handling data. I have omitted solving problems as a heading as this does not lend itself to a separate section here.

The books give ideas for activities to help children learn. Some ideas are more deskbound than others. Many ideas involve children moving around. I suggest materials that teachers can produce, and supply photocopiable resources. There is much of the Numeracy Strategy that is not mentioned in these books. I have concentrated on areas where we have found children in need of a more creative approach. The creativity of early years teaching is not in question. I have been involved in bringing more creativity into the teaching of children in Years 3 to 6 especially.

Many of my colleagues also develop material for their maths classes and have been happy to contribute their ideas. Teachers are constantly on the look-out for ideas to help their children learn. Most are generous with sharing their ideas. I hope that this is another forum for discussion and that we shall all learn together.

Acknowledgements

I would like to thank my colleagues at Fairley House for their help with getting this series together. In particular I would like to thank:

- Elizabeth Morrell for her support in setting up the project and for reading through the final draft;
- Jackie Murray for proof reading and giving helpful suggestions for improvement; and
- the following for allowing me to include their ideas:

    Mark Bolton
    Caroline Lillywhite
    Rosena Mentior
    Iona Mitchell
    Denise Mulholland
    Ann Osborn
    Jeanette Platt
    Joanne Tarr
    Veronica Woolvett

James Bentall helped with copying the photographs.

1 | Number: Introduction

This is not intended to be a sequence of lessons, to be used one after the other. Instead, it is a collection of ideas for helping children to become interested in number, helping them to understand concepts, and engaging them in the learning process in a meaningful and stimulating way. I have given examples of ways in which we have helped children to be interested in and to understand maths. Many of these ideas can be adapted for use at various levels of understanding and development.

Children may have difficulties in the understanding of some areas only. They may fear the very idea of number. They may find the language used difficult to understand and remember, and to associate with concepts. Some children like to learn through deciphering messages on paper; some are stimulated when they receive ticks for their work. However, many others like to move around, to experiment, to discuss. With some children, teachers need to grab their attention with a new activity that will have an element of surprise.

I hope I have included a range of suggestions so that most parents and teachers of children with difficulties in working with number will be able to find something to stimulate these children.

With younger children it is inevitable that practical activities dominate maths lessons. With the pressures of testing and results, teachers often find that they are having to teach what to do and how to do it, having little time for the more creative teaching that we enjoyed in the past. We have found that one well-thought-out practical activity, that includes a lot of discussion and opportunities for children to express their ideas and to be physically as well as mentally involved, can help them make a major discovery, one that would take a lot longer to acquire if presented as a fact or a procedure.

Much of our teaching is concerned with repetition and explanation. Some of it asks the children to learn facts. We hope and believe that a lot of it is fun.

2 Memory Training

Many of the children I teach have difficulty retaining information. This is due to a variety of factors. During their early years children are constantly gaining in knowledge and understanding, and surprise us with how quickly they develop. However, for some children remembering facts and concepts is a difficulty throughout their school life. Most children need memory training as part of their usual school routine. Some need this more than others do. I am including the following ideas here, at an early stage of the book, but they can and should be used throughout the primary school.

Activity 1

▶ Put a variety of objects on a tray and show them to the children for one minute. Remove the tray and ask the children to draw or write down as many of the objects as possible. When the children read out their lists, ask what strategies they used to recall the objects.

▶ Do the same activity using geometric shapes.

▶ Reduce the time the objects are displayed.

Activity 2

▶ Show the children a large sheet with pictures of objects on it (or use an OHP transparency – see Photocopiable Sheet A). Again, show the sheet for one minute, remove and ask children to recall what they saw. Discuss strategies for recall. It is fun to make up your own sheet of objects, including some pictures that have featured in class work recently.

▶ Do the same activity with numbers, using a variety of sizes and colours (see Photocopiable Sheet B, but again, make up your own).

▶ Repeat this with a sheet of geometrical shapes (see Photocopiable Sheet C).

▶ Think of other concepts or ideas that you want the children to revise. For instance, you could make a sheet of sums, using specific mathematical symbols.

In these activities an important part of the exercise is discussing strategies for recall. Many children with learning difficulties will need help in devising such strategies. Other children may say that, with objects or pictures of objects, they put them into categories according to use or family. They may have remembered the initial letters of the objects. They may have looked for connections between various objects. Some may have made up stories. With those children who have not devised such strategies it is important to help them choose one that suits them.

RESOURCES

- Tray
- Variety of objects
- Geometric shapes
- OHP
- Transparent sheet of pictures (Photocopiable Sheet A)
- Transparent sheet of numbers (Photocopiable Sheet B)
- Transparent sheet of shapes (Photocopiable Sheet C)
- Transparent sheet of sums with signs

Photocopiable Sheet A

16   50

15   33

17

66

45   **44**

100   10

1   63

13

47   **65**

32   20

Photocopiable Sheet B

Photocopiable Sheet C

3 Numbers as Digits (1)

Young children often arrive at school counting and writing numbers in a fashion and having some knowledge of adding things together. Some children are already showing a good understanding, but some are having real difficulties. Our dyslexic and dyspraxic children often have difficulties with the fundamental maths activities and concepts. The following are some ideas to help children build up their skills.

Activity 1

Ask children to trace over large numerals, with clearly marked beginnings and ends.

Activity 2

Give the children pictures of numerals and ask them to copy them with plasticine.

Activity 3

Ask children to write numerals in sand and compare with their neighbour.

Activity 4

Ask children to write against a vertical line. This is an idea to help children who persist with reversals while progressing in other areas of number work. (I learned it from Joyce Steeves at a lecture in New York.) With a right-handed child, present the vertical line. Ask the child to write the numbers attached to the right of the line (the side of the line near their writing hand), starting from the line when possible and starting as near as possible to the line otherwise (Figure 3.1).

With left-handed children the instructions include that the child writes on the side away from his or her writing side.

I developed this idea a step further with a right-handed child. I handed him a ruler and asked him to hold this vertically on a paper in front of him and to write his numerals against the side of it. This was a great success and he could grab his ruler and practise at any odd moment. This method is not possible for a left-handed child.

Figure 3.1: Writing numbers against a vertical line

RESOURCES
- Tracing paper
- Sand tray
- Plasticine
- Pencils
- Paper
- Rulers

4 Numbers as Digits (2)

Children often learn to chant numbers in order, but have little idea of the meaning of their words. They may also write numerals, but be unsure about their meaning. Numerals are displayed in the classroom with pictures to illustrate their meaning. During all the common activities children tend to pick up their meaning. However, for a few children, the attachment of a meaningful and remembered label is a real difficulty.

It is useful to display patterns of numbers. Most children are familiar with the arrangements of the dots on dice or dominoes. Display these and use them to break down numbers (Figure 4.1).

Figure 4.1: Arrangement of dots (1 to 6) on dice or dominoes

For instance, 2 can be seen as 1 and 1. If you use the above array of dots for 3, it can be seen as 1 and 2. 4 is seen as two lots of 2. 5 is made up of 2 and 3. 6 is two sets of 3 or three sets of 2. You need to produce dot arrays for the numbers 7 to 10. These should look like Figure 4.2.

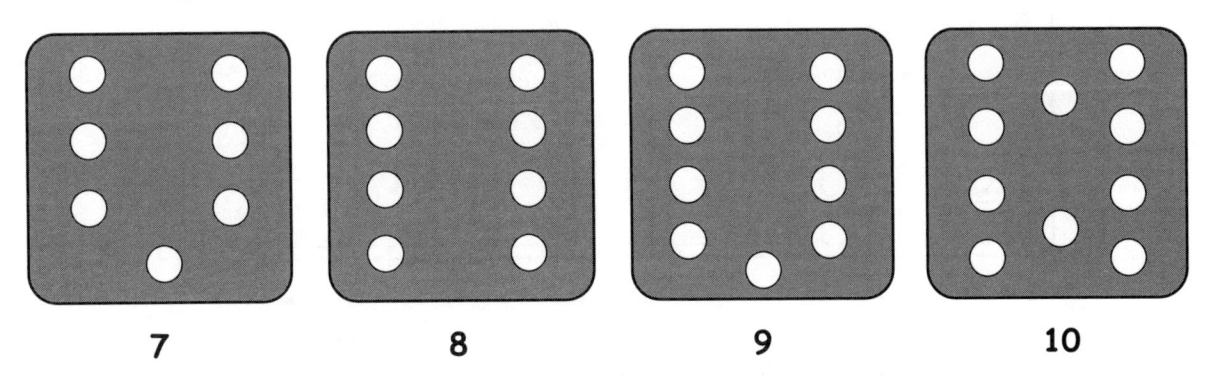

Figure 4.2: Arrangement of dots for numbers 7 to 10

7 is made up of 4 and 3 or 6 and 1. 8 is two sets of 4 or four sets of 2. 9 is 5 and 4, and 10 is 5 and 5.

As the children get used to these arrays you can introduce different number combinations to develop work on number bonds.

5　Number Bonds and Beach Huts

One of my colleagues was working with our very youngest children, aged six and seven, teaching them number bonds. She knew that they learned more when they were actively involved, and constantly invented games to help them understand number. This is one that her group loved and that helped them to learn number bonds to 10.

She used a cardboard box measuring 1 m 30 cm long, 90 cm high and 15 cm deep. She then cut out beach huts starting on the left side with one which could hold one plastic cup, the next could hold two cups, one on top of the other, and she continued in this way to the beach hut that would hold ten cups (Figure 5.1).

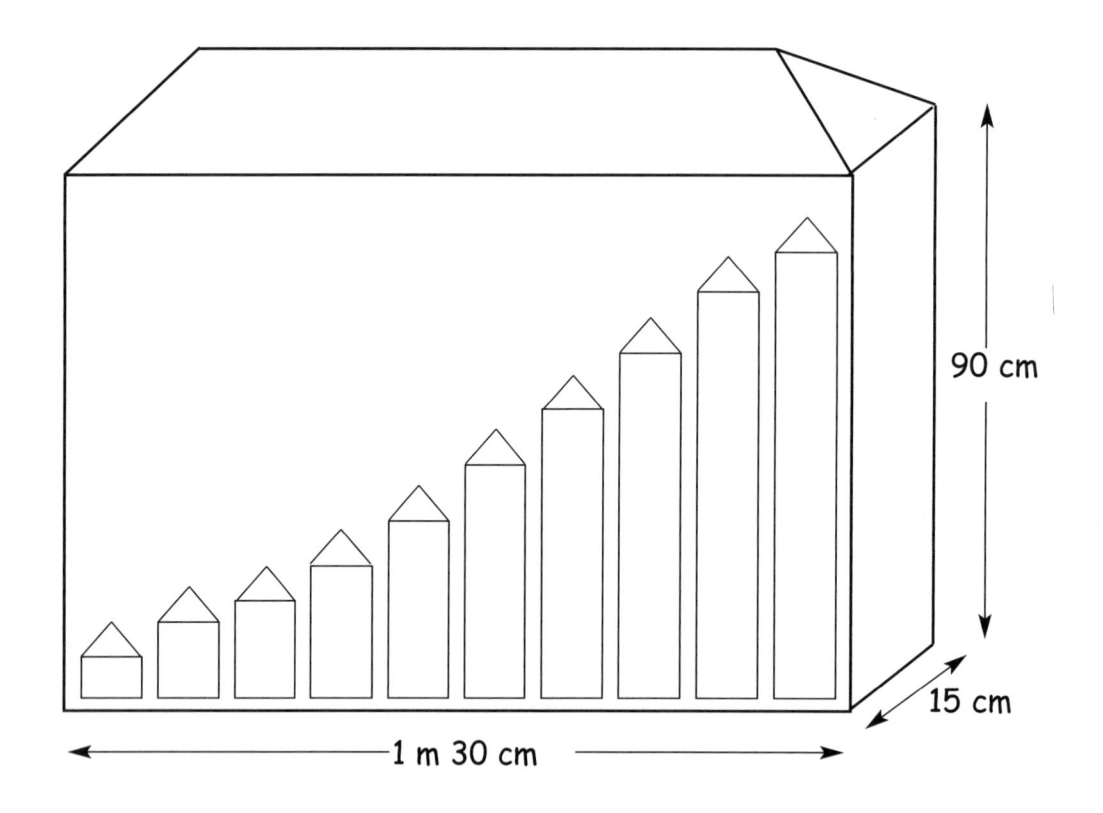

Figure 5.1: Beach huts model for teaching number bonds

The children decorated each cup to look like a different 'person' and stuck a circular piece of card on the bottom of the cups so that the cups could be stacked and held together with Blu-Tack and to reinforce the concept of 2s, 3s etc. as opposed to thinking of numbers in a unitary sense.

The cup people then had a party in a chosen beach hut. The cup people were allowed into the party in two groups, but only if the two groups filled up the beach hut. For example, if there were to be a party at number 10, the groups allowed in would be 9 and 1, 8 and 2, 7 and 3, and so on. (There would have to be two sets of five available for the 5 and 5 number bond.)

The children took it in turns to take enough plastic-cup people to a party at number 10 to fill it up. One child took the set of four cups from hut number 4 and the set of six from hut number 6. Placing these on top of each other ensured that they fitted number 10 exactly. They then took it in turns to find other pairs. (The teacher had made another set of five, ready for when a child chose the 5 set.)

This proved a very popular game and the children soon learned their number bonds.

RESOURCES

- Cardboard box
- Plastic cups to fit spaces
- Circular pieces of card (to fit the bottom of the cups)
- Blu-Tack

6 Teaching Number Bonds by Wearing Silly Hats

Once children have learned the names and value of numbers up to 20, they need to be able to use them to count and then to combine totals. Not all children find it easy to combine numbers quickly, to be able to quickly work out totals of two numbers and then learn the number bonds to 10 and to 20.

To be able to add and subtract mentally, children need to build up pictures in their mind. They need to be able to 'see' the quantities they are working with, in their head and not on the table or floor. It is this internalisation of numbers and number values that is the most difficult stage of learning for many young children.

Most children love learning by moving around. They also learn when having fun. The following describes a successful method that I invented and that I have used with many children.

The games I describe below are ways I have used the hats. I am sure that others will be able to think of many other ways, including using the hats, to practise larger number bonds and multiplication and division.

THE HAT GAMES

Activity 1

Ask the children to each choose a hat, put it on their head and say the number. Ask each child in turn to pick up a number card and add the number on it to the number on their head. What is the total? This game encourages the children to remember the first number, as, when it is on their head they cannot see it. At first they will soon forget the number once it is on their head, but will soon begin to remember the number without taking a second peep. This is good memory training.

Activity 2

Give some children the hats and others the number cards. Each child with a hat has to find a child with a number card that will give a certain total when added to the number on their hat. For example, ask the child with 6 on their hat to find a child with a card with the number on it which, added to theirs, will make a total of, say, 9. Play this game lots of times, so that children find all the number bonds to 10.

Activity 3

Use all the hats and ask the children to find a partner, so that the total of the numbers on their hats will be 10. (You will need the two 5s for this game.) They will soon begin to remember some of the pairs.

Activity 4

Put the hats on the children so that they cannot see the number. Give each one a card with a number and dots on it. Tell each child the total of the number in their hand and the number on their head and ask them to work out the number on their hat.

Activity 5

Give out all the hats and numbers to different children. The children with hats can look at their numbers before putting on the hats. Say a number and ask each child to find a partner (one with a hat, one with a card) so that their numbers combine to make a certain total. The winners are the children who sit down in a pair first.

Activity 6

Give out all the hats and numbers to different children. Say a number and ask each child with a card to find a partner with a hat to make a certain total. The winners are the children who sit down in a pair first.

Activity 7

Make more hats with numbers up to 20 and use these to play games similar to the ones above. You can stick the larger numbers (11 to 20) over the lower ones, or make new hats and use all the numbers 0 to 20. If you stick numbers over the old ones, put 11 on the 1 hat, 12 on the 2 hat and so on. This gives you a good opportunity to tackle place value.

RESOURCES

- Twelve hats (each one different from the others, numerals from 0 to 10, with two number 5s)
- Eleven cards with numerals 0 to 10 (each with matching dot pattern – preferably like those found on dominoes or dice)

14 *Number*

7 Number Bonds with an Addition Square

Activity

Ask the children to complete the addition square (Photocopiable Sheet D). Ask them to look at the patterns. What do they notice? There are many opportunities for discussion about sequences and patterns, about the effects of adding one more, and about logic. Children should be encouraged to use as many words associated with addition as possible. Children could be given points (or rewards) for each time they use a new expression, e.g. 'The sum of the numbers in the 3 column is 30 more than the sum of the numbers in the 1 column.'

Rehearse directions on the square before you begin to ask specific questions about the square. For instance, do the children remember the meaning of the words 'horizontal' and 'vertical'? Can they indicate a diagonal?

Examples of questions you could ask:

1. Are there any particular patterns that you can see?
2. What do you notice about the diagonals?
3. How many totals have two digits?
4. What are the horizontal and vertical patterns?

Each question should be accompanied by the further question, 'Why?'

RESOURCES

- Addition square (Photocopiable Sheet D)
- Pencils
- Rubbers
- Counting equipment

(A set of laminated addition squares can be used and reused with OHP pens.)

Addition Square

+	1	2	3	4	5	6	7	8	9	10
1										
2										
3										
4										
5										
6										
7										
8										
9										
10										

Photocopiable Sheet D

8 Number Bonds with a Difference Square

Activity

Ask the children to complete the difference square (Photocopiable Sheet E). This is used in the same way as an addition square. Start by reading the first number in the horizontal line, finding the difference between this and the first number in the vertical line. The difference between 10 and 10 is 0. Write this number in the appropriate square. Then find the difference between the second number in the horizontal line and the first number in the vertical line. The difference between 9 and 10 is 1.

The calculations can be done in any order, although you might like to demonstrate using a structured approach to begin with. Later on you could highlight some squares and ask the children to find the differences for these squares only.

You should ask the children to study the patterns made, and to tell you what they notice. This gives many opportunites for discussion about sequences and patterns, about the effects of deducting one more, about logic.

You should try to use as many words associated with subtraction as possible. You could give children points (or rewards) for each time they use a new expression (e.g. difference, minus, take away, deduct, decrease).

Examples of questions you could ask:

1. Are there any particular patterns that you can see?
2. What do you notice about the diagonals?
3. How many times does each digit appear in the answers?
4. What are the horizontal and vertical patterns?

Each question should be accompanied by the further question, 'Why?'

RESOURCES

- Difference square (Photocopiable Sheet E)
- Pencils
- Rubbers
- Counting equipment

(A set of laminated difference squares can be used and reused with OHP pens.)

Difference Square

-	10	9	8	7	6	5	4	3	2	1
10										
9										
8										
7										
6										
5										
4										
3										
2										
1										

Photocopiable Sheet E

9 Place Value with Early Learners

A teacher of our very early learners, mostly children of six years, has worked hard to give her children an understanding of mathematics. Over the years she has had to work in a multitude of ways to try to get each of these very individual children to gain some concept of number. Below are some of the ideas that have succeeded. Some are adapted from Ginn and Heinemann games. This teacher has adapted the games to ensure that her children get rewards for their own efforts and has eliminated some of the competitive elements.

Activity 1: Number bonds to 10

You need counters, a die, cards numbered 0 to 10 and a card like that in Photocopiable Sheet F with stars in some of the squares. You can scan a picture onto the sheet to make it more exciting and appeal to the interests of the group.

Children choose a counter and put their counter on **Start**. They take it in turns to throw the die and move their counter that number of squares in any direction. If they land on a star they take one of the numbered cards (turned upside down in a pile). If they can say the number on the card and the amount that must be added to it to make 10, they get a star or a special sticker.

The game can be extended to practise number bonds to 20 or more.

Activity 2: Sequencing numbers: largest to smallest and smallest to largest

You need counters, a die, several small packs of numbered cards (e.g. 1, 8 and 10; 2, 9 and 5) and a card as in Photocopiable Sheet F.

Children choose a counter and put their counter on **Start**. They take it in turns to throw the die and move their counter that number of squares in any direction. If they land on a star they choose a number pack. They then arrange the numbers in order (either smallest to largest or largest to smallest) to win a star or special sticker.

The game can be extended so that larger numbers are used. Language can be built up over time: largest, greatest, smallest, least, most, etc.

Activity 3: Doubles

You need counters, a die, cards numbered 1 to 10 and a card like the one in Photocopiable Sheet G. Place the numbered cards face down on the table.

Children choose a counter and put their counter on **Start**. They take it in turns to throw the die and move their counter that number of squares in any direction. If they land on a star they choose a number card. If they can double it they win a reward.

An extension is to ask for an immediate response. Differentiation can be useful as you can take into account the level of learning the child has reached and vary the expectations.

Activity 4: Counting on from the largest digit

As all teachers know, this is often one of the most difficult things to get children to do. You will need a picture board as in Photocopiable Sheet G, counters and two spotted dice.

Children choose a counter and put their counter on **Start**. They take it in turns to throw the dice and total the two numbers by counting on from the largest. If they get the correct total through the correct method, they move their counter that number of squares in any direction. If they land on a star they get a reward.

An extension is to use one numbered die and one spotted die. A further extension is to use just numbered die.

Activity 5: Using money to practise counting in 10s

Look at a 100 square (Photocopiable Sheet F) and show the children how to count in tens. Ask children to join in.

Give each child a bunch of 10p coins to count aloud to the group (starting with two or three coins). If they are correct they get a reward.

Put sets of 10p coins in small boxes ('Oxo' boxes are ideal and can be covered in attractive paper). Put varying numbers of 10p coins in the boxes. Ask the children in turn to choose a box and open it. They then have to count out the 10s to the group. If they are correct they get a reward.

As an extension, point out the 10s on the 100 square and ask the children to place their piles on the correct number.

A further extension is to put 10p and 1p coins in the boxes and ask the children to count out the tens and ones.

RESOURCES

- Counters
- Cards numbered 0 to 10
- Adhesive stars
- Plastic 10p and 1p coins
- Dice (some with numbers and some with spots)
- Photocopiable Sheet F
- 100 squares (Photocopiable Sheet F)
- Small boxes

1	2	3	4	5	6	7	8	9	10
11	12	13	14	15	16	17	18	19	20
21	22	23	24	25	26	27	28	29	30
31	32	33	34	35	36	37	38	39	40
41	42	43	44	45	46	47	48	49	50
51	52	53	54	55	56	57	58	59	60
61	62	63	64	65	66	67	68	69	70
71	72	73	74	75	76	77	78	79	80
81	82	83	84	85	86	87	88	89	90
91	92	93	94	95	96	97	98	99	100

Photocopiable Sheet F

Start

Photocopiable Sheet G

10 Bonds and Loops

Children should use a variety of strategies when practising mental arithmetic. Some they discover for themselves, but it is often necessary for you to lead them to the most efficient (for them) method of working. I have found that concentration on number bonds is important and necessary as a means of helping children to retain and use information without overloading the memory.

When given a list of numbers to add together, I teach children to look for number bonds and loop these together. For instance,

$$25 + 36 + 12 + 24 + 45 + 38$$

First, the 10s are added together. Going from left to right, we have 20 + 30 is 50. Add 10 gives 60. Continue to the end and we have 150. Then, the numbers in the 1s place are looped to make groups of ten, which, added together, give us 30. We then add the 150 and the 30 to give 180.

The children could use two different colours or dotted and solid lines if the teacher decided to use number bonds in the 10s place. For instance:

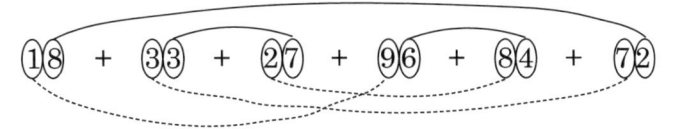

$$18 + 33 + 27 + 96 + 84 + 72$$

Frequent practice with these types of looped additions helps children develop their ability to use number bonds and their memory skills.

RESOURCES

- Sheet of linear addition sums (Photocopiable Sheet H)
- Pencils
- One or two coloured pencils

Bonds and Loops

Loop digits to join numbers which are easy to add together.

1.   26 + 37 + 15 + 14 + 23

2.   126 + 58 + 34 + 13 + 17 + 22

3.   55 + 44 + 13 + 26 + 36 + 45

4.   49 + 55 + 11 + 38 + 2 + 25

5.   13 + 28 + 17 + 32 + 33

6.   56 + 21 + 33 + 19 + 24 + 27

Photocopiable Sheet H

11 Place Value: The Mushroom Story

Many children with mathematical learning difficulties find it difficult to understand the concept of place value and, as they get older, need new experiences. The following has worked well with dyslexic children I have taught.

Activity

Give each child a place value mat (Photocopiable Sheet I).

Tell them the mushroom story: You are going out to collect mushrooms. Each time that mushrooms are mentioned in the story, the children must tally them in the 1s column. They do not need to use the other columns at this stage. You could start thus: I am in a field and I see a clump of four mushrooms, and I pick them. Behind a tree I find seven more. Over a stile I find a beautiful clump of eight mushrooms. (The children should now have tallied as in Figure 11.1.) You can continue this story to any number. Children count in 5s to say how many mushrooms they have collected.

100s	10s	1s

Figure 11.1: Place value mat used as a tally sheet – stage 1

You then ask if there could be any easier way to tally and count. You should lead the children to the suggestion that they could cross off or rub out groups of ten and put a

25

tally mark in the 10s column. In the above example they would have ended up with one tally mark in the 10s column and nine left in the 1s column (Figure 11.2).

100s	10s	1s
	|	̶|̶|̶|̶|̶ ||||

Figure 11.2: Place value mat used as a tally sheet – stage 2

They could then substitute these marks for numbers and read off the total (Figure 11.3).

100s	10s	1s
	1	9

Figure 11.3: Place value mat used as a tally sheet – stage 3

The action of transferring groups helps the children to appreciate the value of the columns.

Playing this game has helped a lot of children to a better understanding of place value. Altering the story to pick apples in an orchard or collect ants in a jar keeps the interest going.

RESOURCES

- Place value mats (Photocopiable Sheet I, copied and laminated)
- OHP pens
- Tissues for rubbing out

100s	10s	1s

Photocopiable Sheet I

12 Place Value: Column Addition

Using a place value mat like that shown as Photocopiable Sheet I helps children who are still using concrete equipment to understand column addition.

100s	10s	1s
	2	8
	1	6

Figure 12.1: Place value mat used for column addition

In the above example (Figure 12.1) the children are asked to add 28 and 16. They need Multilink cubes, two sets of ten, joined together, in the 10s column on top of the number 2 and one set of ten on top of the number 1. They then need eight single Multilink in the 1s column with six more under them. They count the Multilink in the 1s column and, when they get 14, split these into one set of ten and four 1s. Put the four 1s in the 1s column 'answer box' and the set of ten in the 10s column under the 'answer box'. Collect all sets of ten and put them in the 'answer box'. Describe what we now have. There are four 10s and four 1s. Move the Multilink and write the numbers. We can read this as 44.

This is an extension of work done earlier, with the children using the place value mats to ensure that they are fully aware of the notion of grouping and exchange.

This should be done before tackling the use of numbers only.

RESOURCES

- Multilink
- Tissues to rub out
- OHP pens
- Place value mats (Photocopiable Sheet I, copied and laminated)

13 Place Value: Standard Algorithm

Using a place value mat like that shown as Photocopiable Sheet I helps children to understand column addition using a standard algorithm.

100s	10s	1s
	5	8
	7	7
		15

Figure 13.1: Place value mat used for standard algorithm

In the above example (Figure 13.1) the children are asked to add 58 and 77. They start by adding the numbers in the 1s column. They get 15. Ask them to write this number at the bottom of the column as above. Discuss the two digits and, as they understand that they have a ten and five 1s, they can transfer the 5 to the 'answer box' in the 1s column. The 10 can then be placed under the 'answer box' of the 10s column. The original 15 is then rubbed out. The children then add the 10s, and get, including the carried ten, 13 10s. Discuss what to do with this number in the same way as you did with the 15.

The action of writing the totals in the column being considered helps the children to understand the process. Rubbing out and transferring helps them to understand the algorithm.

RESOURCES

- Place value mats (Photocopiable Sheet H, copied and laminated)
- OHP pens
- Tissues for rubbing out

14 Place Value: Column Subtraction

A place value mat like that shown as Photocopiable Sheet I also helps children who are still using concrete equipment to understand column subtraction.

100s	10s	1s
	8	4
	5	8

Figure 14.1: Place value mat used for column subtraction

In the above example (Figure 14.1) the children are asked to subtract 58 from 84. As in the previous example, the children can use sets of tens of Multilink and separate cubes. Place on the mat as before. Start with the 1s column. 4 take away 8, we cannot do. Take one of the eight sets of 10 from the 10s column and place it in the 1s column with the 1s. You can now take away the eight 1s from the 14 1s above. Write the answer in the 'answer box'. Continue to solve the 10s column, placing the answer in the 'answer box'.

Extend the children's understanding by omitting the use of Multilink and discussing the standard algorithm. This time, when decomposing, take a 10 from the eight 10s by rubbing out the 8 and replacing with 7 and adding ten to the 4 in the 1s column, thus giving 14. By studying this, the children can see that 70 add 14 is the same as 80 add 4 – we have just rearranged the numbers.

RESOURCES

- Multilink
- Tissues for rubbing out
- OHP pens
- Place value mats (Photocopiable Sheet I, copied and laminated)

15 | Place Value: Whole Numbers and Decimals

A laminated card, as illustrated in Photocopiable Sheet J, can be used to teach and practise several concepts. This can be written on with some felt-tipped pens and most OHP pens. This means that the cards can be used and reused, and that children do not mind 'having a go', as mistakes can be wiped off. There are many uses for teachers.

- Use to discuss place value of two- or three-digit numbers. For example, 124 can be read from the card as one 100, two 10s, four 1s. This can lead to a discussion of how you would read the number 124 without the headings.
- Use to discuss decimal place. Each column has a value ten times bigger or smaller than the one to each side. Discuss the whole number columns first. Start at the 100s column and discuss how the column to the right has a value ten times smaller. The one to its right again has a value ten times smaller. What is ten times smaller than 1?
- You can extend the above by using a large decimal point which is held by a child. Other children hold digits and range themselves round the decimal point to make a number, e.g. 23.4. What happens if we make this number ten times bigger (multiply this number by ten)? The child holding the dot does not move, but the ones on either

side move up a place. Now the number can be read as 234. The same activity can be done in reverse to illustrate a number becoming ten times smaller (dividing by ten).
- Add the £ sign to the first three columns. Discuss the decimal point when writing sums of money. Ask the children to write down £324.42. Ask them the value of each column.
- Use to explain metres and centimetres, kilograms and grams.

RESOURCES

- Laminated board (Photocopiable Sheet J)
- Marker pens
- Tissues for rubbing out

1000s	100s	10s	1s	1/10s	1/100s

Photocopiable Sheet J

16 Missing Number Calculations

Many children have difficulties in understanding and solving 'missing number' calculations. One reason for this is that usually the first linear calculations they see are of this type: 2 + 3 = 5, 4 + 5 = 9. They learn that this is the 'right' way to do things, and then, suddenly, they are asked to solve

$$5 + \Box = 9 \text{ or } \Box - 5 = 5.$$

What children need is experience of the variety of ways of communicating in mathematics, from as early a stage as possible.

It is important to do a lot of work on the meaning of equality and balance. Discuss how balances work and give children concrete tools, such as Multilink or a number line. With questions such as

$$\Box - 14 = 12$$

a picture such as that in Figure 16.1 is useful.

Use the balance sheet in Figure 16.2 to give the children practice in thinking about the logic of the signs, and reading them so that the sentences make sense. For instance, with the above example, the questions would be, 'What did I have to begin with, if I took away 14 and had 12 left?'

RESOURCES

- Multilink
- Balances
- Number lines
- 100 squares (see Photocopiable Sheet F)
- Picture (see Figure 16.1)
- Balance sheets (see Figure 16.2)

Missing Number Calculations   35

What was in the bag to begin with if you take out 14 and 12 are left?

☐ − 14 = 12

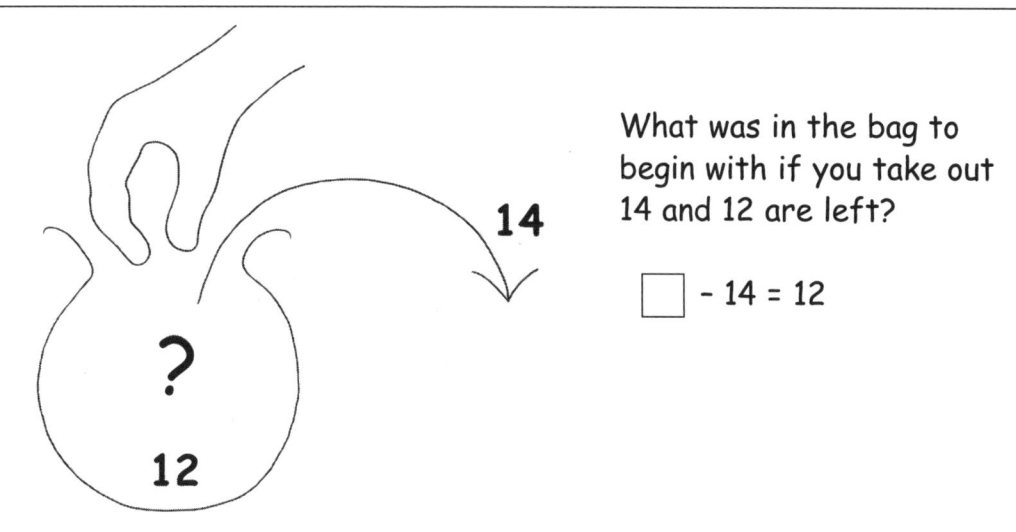

Figure 16.1: What was in the bag?

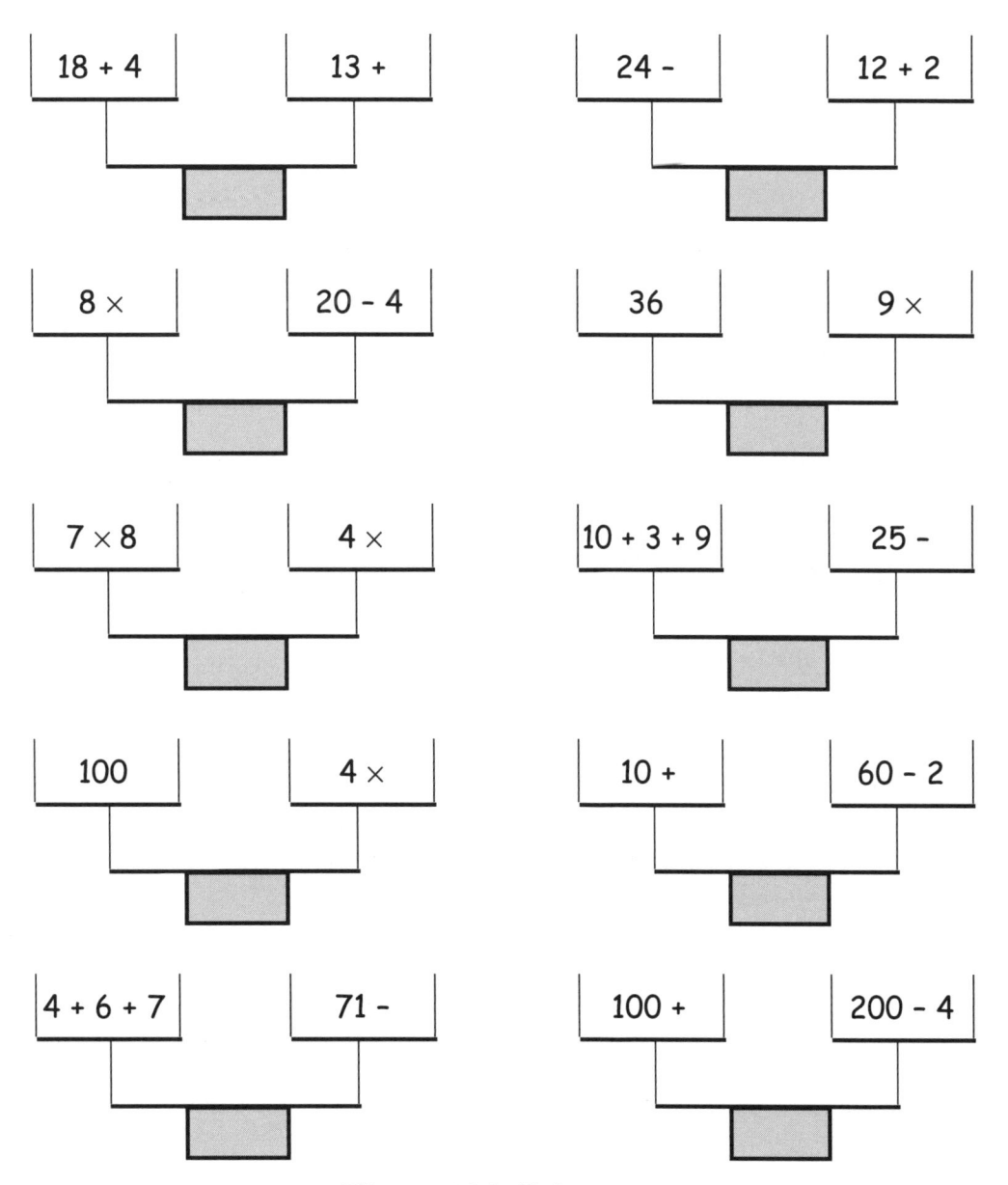

18 + 4	13 +		24 −	12 + 2
8 ×	20 − 4		36	9 ×
7 × 8	4 ×		10 + 3 + 9	25 −
100	4 ×		10 +	60 − 2
4 + 6 + 7	71 −		100 +	200 − 4

Figure 16.2: Balance sums

17 Bingo

There are many commercial bingo games for use in the classroom. We enjoy using a lot of them and practising our four rules of number (+, −, ×, ÷. This bingo game is one I made up some years ago when I first started working with dyslexic children. We were doing a lot of work using 100 squares and I was interested in how difficult some of these children found it to understand the layout and then to remember the place of numbers on the square. This game is intended to get the children to really think about the square and the place of numbers on it (and why the numbers are where they are).

▶ Activity

Take a blank 100 square (Photocopiable Sheet K) and fill in a certain quantity of the numbers in the position they would be found on a 100 square. I chose to put 18 numbers on each card, but you can use more or fewer than these. Laminate the cards. (Alternatively laminate copies of Photocopiable Sheets L to N.) Cut up a completed 100 square into its 100 squares and put these in a box.

Give each child a card with numbers on it, but a different one from that of his or her neighbour. Each child also needs a marker pen.

You take a square out of the box one at a time and call out the number on the square. If a child has this number he or she colours it in (or puts a dot or cross on it). The first child to correctly complete his or her card is the winner.

If you have another adult handy he or she could be marking off the numbers you call on another 100 square, so that checking is easy. Alternatively, dispense with the cut-up square and shut your eyes and stab numbers on a 100 square to call numbers. This way you have the record yourself.

Children soon begin to become more efficient at finding the numbers on their cards. You can discuss this with them.

RESOURCES

- Set of numbered cards (Photocopiable Sheets L to N, copied and laminated)
- Marker pens
- Box of numbers and/or 100 square (Photocopiable Sheet K)

Photocopiable Sheet K

Grid 1

		3			6				10
	12	14						19	
						27			
	32				36			39	
				45					
			54						60
61						67			
					76				
	82								
					96				

Grid 2

		3			6		8		
			14		16				
	22								
				35					
41							48		
			54						60
61						67			
		73							
					86				90
	92						98		

Photocopiable Sheet L

Grid 1

1			4			7			
	12				16				
21							28		
31				35					
			44						
					56				60
61								69	
				75					
	82								
		93					98		

Grid 2

1				5					10
	12				16				
21							28		
31				35					
			44						
					56			59	
61								69	
				75					
	82								
		93				97			

Photocopiable Sheet M

Grid 1

1			4						10
11								19	
				25		27			
31					36				
		43							
						57			
	62			65					
					76				80
		83							
		93							100

Grid 2

1						6		8		
				14			17			
		22			25					
			33							
41						46		48		
				54						
	62						67			70
		73								
					85					
							97			

Photocopiable Sheet N

18 The 100 Square

This is one of the most important of tools in helping children count, understand place value, hone their memory skills, learn number bonds, investigate percentages, and look at fractions. Children may arrive in our schools with very little concept of the structure of the number system. Number words may be chanted, but values not understood. Mental arithmetic cannot be learned, understood and used unless there is a mental image on which to hang ideas. Every time I think I have used the 100 square in just about every way I can think of, I learn about another.

Most 100 squares are printed with the 0 or 1 in the top left-hand corner and the other numbers continuing along and down the square. I am going to suggest that teachers use the square shown in Photocopiable Sheet O for a lot of their work with numbers. I like it because the values of the digits grow from the bottom to the top of the square. As will be seen later, some ideas are better explored with a 100 square starting with 1. However, it is important that children learn early on to respect the number 0, and I like the idea that it takes pride of place in this square, anchoring a corner and being the first number. Ideas for use and the development of other concepts can be seen on subsequent pages.

Activity 1: Explore the 100 square

▶ Children count from 0, pointing to each number as they say it. With younger children, teachers can concentrate on lower values first, gradually moving up the square.

▶ Explore the second figure (the 1s place) in each square along two consecutive rows. What can you notice?

▶ Extend this to include other rows. Eventually look at the whole square.

▶ Read the numbers in the 10s place along two consecutive rows (reading first as one 10, two 10s, three 10s and so on, and then translating to 10, 20, 30). Extend this to more rows, to the whole square. What do you notice? (Starting the 100 square with 0 ensures that the 10s figure in each row remains the same. If you start with 1 you have a different 10s figure at the end of each row, e.g. the number at the end of the third row would be 30.)

▶ Use OHP pens to highlight any of the above activities and to look for patterns. Highlight the 10s in one column. Compare with the 10s in another column. What do you notice? Why?

90	91	92	93	94	95	96	97	98	99
80	81	82	83	84	85	86	87	88	89
70	71	72	73	74	75	76	77	78	79
60	61	62	63	64	65	66	67	68	69
50	51	52	53	54	55	56	57	58	59
40	41	42	43	44	45	46	47	48	49
30	31	32	33	34	35	36	37	38	39
20	21	22	23	24	25	26	27	28	29
10	11	12	13	14	15	16	17	18	19
0	1	2	3	4	5	6	7	8	9

Photocopiable Sheet O

▶ Choose a diagonal line (e.g. 50, 41, 32, 23, 14, 5). What changes in the 10s column? What changes in the 1s column? Why?

▶ Choose a square of numbers and highlight. Compare diagonally arranged numbers.

RESOURCES

- Laminated 100 square for each child (Photocopiable Sheet O).
- OHP or water-based pens.

Activity 2: Number bonds using the 100 square

Children will be learning number bonds to 10 and 20 using a variety of activities, as mentioned earlier in this book. Teachers should refer to addition and subtraction bonds, as I feel it is inefficient to learn one without the other. Children often find it more difficult to remember and use the number bonds to 50 or 100. The 100 square helps with this.

▶ Look at the bottom row. Loop the numbers that are bonds to 10, using different coloured highlighters for each bond (9 and 1, 8 and 2, etc.).

▶ See how quickly you can see and say the bonds to 20 (19 and 1, 18 and 2, etc.) Can you see where each pair is compared with the pairs to 10?

▶ Try the pairs to 30. What happens after they reach 20 and 10?

▶ With number bonds to 50 and then 100 the same patterns and rules apply.

▶ It is easy to follow the addition bonds with the subtraction bonds. The connections can clearly be seen.

▶ What happens if we now add 100 to each of our patterns? For instance, we can see that 26 and 24 make 50. What do we add to 126 to make 150?

▶ Experiment with different ways of using highlighters. The children can connect with arrows. They can fill in groups of squares.

▶ Have speed tests where appropriate. 'Find the number that must be added to 19 to make 30. Join the two numbers.'

RESOURCES

- Laminated 100 square for each child (Photocopiable Sheet O).
- OHP or water-based pens.

Activity 3: Explore fractions, decimals and percentages using the 100 square

This is when it is preferable to use the 100 square that starts with 1, as printed in Photocopiable Sheet P.

Make sure that you have enough for two laminated 100 squares for each child.

▶ Ask the children to start at 1 and colour half of the 100 squares red, starting at 1 and colouring consecutive squares. They will have coloured 50 out of 100. 50 is half of 100. They have coloured in 50/100 or half. Show them a % sign and explain that this means 'out of 100'. Looking at the 100 square they will see that a half is 50 out of 100, or 50%.

▶ Ask the children to colour blue half of what is left, starting at 51 and colouring consecutive numbers. They will have coloured in the numbers 51 to 75 inclusive. Can the children notice anything about the square now? They should see that they have coloured in 25 squares in blue, leaving 25 uncoloured. 25 is half of 50. They can see that there are four 25s in 100 and so each section is a quarter (one out of four or one-quarter) of the whole; it is 25 out of 100; it is 25%.

▶ Try other fractions. For example, colour 20 squares red, 20 blue, 20 yellow, 20 green and 20 purple. Each section is one out of five or one-fifth. It is also 20 out of 100 or 20%.

▶ Use two 100-square cards to demonstrate the decimal point. Each card is a whole. Ask the children to colour in the numbers 1 to 50 on the second card. Discuss how they might express a whole one and the 50 out of a 100. Ideas should include one and a half, one whole and 50 out of 100 bits of the second. Give each child a laminated card as shown on page 33.

They have one whole square and 50/100s, as shown in Figure 18.1. Put in the decimal point to explain that the numbers before the decimal point express the number of wholes, and the numbers after express the fractions, percentages, decimal places.

1000s	100s	10s	1/10s	1/100s
		1 ●	5	0

Figure 18.1: Place value mat used to explore decimals

▶ Ask the children to use the laminated cards to write a series of numbers. Start with 2.25. This is two wholes, two-tenths and five-hundredths. It is also two whole ones and 25% of another whole one. It is 2.25.

Children will need a lot of experience of these exercises in order for them to see the connection between fractions, decimals and percentages.

RESOURCES

- Two laminated 100 squares per child (Photocopiable Sheet P)
- OHP pens
- Laminated number card (p. 33)

91	92	93	94	95	96	97	98	99	100
81	82	83	84	85	86	87	88	89	90
71	72	73	74	75	76	77	78	79	80
61	62	63	64	65	66	67	68	69	70
51	52	53	54	55	56	57	58	59	60
41	42	43	44	45	46	47	48	49	50
31	32	33	34	35	36	37	38	39	40
21	22	23	24	25	26	27	28	29	30
11	12	13	14	15	16	17	18	19	20
1	2	3	4	5	6	7	8	9	10

Photocopiable Sheet P

Number

Activity 4: Fun with a 100 square using felt mats

The children enjoy this team game, using a 100 square made up of numbered felt mats, available from various educational suppliers.

- ▶ Divide the children into two teams.
- ▶ Give each member of a team six mats, randomly selected.
- ▶ As the children use up their mats, they can take six more, until all mats are used and the 100 square is laid out correctly.
- ▶ Ask the children to lay out the 100 square on the floor. The children must not talk to each other! They can pick up already-laid mats if they think they are in the wrong place.
- ▶ Time how long the team takes.
- ▶ Repeat the exercise with the second team. The winner is the team that takes the shortest time.
- ▶ Discuss tactics. Encourage children to talk about patterns of the rows and columns.

This game can be used with Key Stage 2 children of any age. The least able can be given help and hints. With the most able, the emphasis can be on speed. It is a good way of helping children to think more about the structure of the 100 square. They also begin to add and subtract in 10s and 1s in a very informal way. They learn to cooperate, to question their actions and to correct errors.

RESOURCES

- 100 square made up of 100 felt mats

19 Fractions

This is another of those concepts that many children find it difficult to grasp. They believe there is some mystique attached to the word. The first thing to do is to demystify the subject. What does the word 'fraction' mean? Ask the children to tell you. When I do this, I get replies like: 'It's a quarter.' 'It means a half.' 'It means you divide it.' (That last one is quite sophisticated.)

Start with getting the language right. Ask the children to think of sentences including the words 'fraction' or 'fractions'. There must be no numbers in this sentence. They find this a difficult task. You need to demonstrate. 'Can I have a fraction of your cake?' 'You are a fraction late.' Ask the children to think about what was happening in both these instances. Eventually, the children will define 'fraction' as meaning 'a bit of'. We can then go on to say that in maths we normally talk about equal fractions and so we can say we split something into two parts, three parts, four parts and so on. Each part is a bit of the whole.

Look at the way we write fractions. $^1/_2$ means one out of two, that is one piece out of the two that make up the whole. Refer to the way teachers mark mental arithmetic tests. 17/20 means you got 17 right out of the 20 questions or parts that made up the test.

It is tempting to use squares and circles initially when teaching about fractions. I think that teachers should resist this. The following activities are intended to help the children build up their own language to explain the concepts.

Activity 1

- Give each child a biscuit (the more crumbly the better) and ask them to break it into two equal halves. Some children will initially be happy with two pieces of different sizes. Point out that the pieces are not equal and ask what the children can do about it. They could try breaking bits off one piece to add to the other. They could weigh their biscuit and share it out. There are many solutions to this, with emphasis always on *equality*.
- Repeat the exercise, asking the children to break their biscuits into four equal pieces. Again, they will find this difficult, but the very act of trying to make each bit equal to the others will help them to internalise the meaning of 'equal fractions'.

Activity 2

Give the children two beakers and a jug of water. Ask them to share the water between the two beakers, so that each beaker has half the quantity. Trial and error is the impor-

48 *Number*

tant process here. The discussion that results helps the children understand the ideas of *sharing* and *equivalence*.

Activity 3

Give each child eight pieces of Multilink, all the same colour. Ask them to make a bar with their Multilink. Now ask them to break this bar in half. Can they explain what they now have? They have two equal pieces. They also have four pieces of Multilink out of eight.

Activity 4

Give them eight pieces of Multilink, ensuring that four are one colour, two another and two another (e.g. red, blue, green). Ask them to make a bar, placing like colours together. Most will end up with four matching, followed by the two sets of two. Now ask them to describe their bar. Lead the children to use these expressions: 'Four out of my eight pieces are red, two out of eight are blue, and two out of eight are green.' They can then break up the bar into colours and see that four out of eight is one-half, two out of eight is one-quarter. What they have is a half, a quarter and a quarter, making a whole.

Activity 5

- Ask the children to make a shape on squared paper, that encloses 12 whole squares. The finished shape must not be a rectangle. Ask them to colour in half of their squares. This should ensure a lively discussion about which squares to fill in, whether they have to be next to each other and how you can find half a shape that is not regular. I have found this a useful activity and one that can be used on a computer using EXCEL.
- Repeat the above, but this time asking the children to fill in half one colour and quarter another colour.
- Vary the instructions, using shapes enclosing, for example, 16 squares (if you want to explore halves, quarters and three-quarters) or 15 (if you want to explore thirds).

Activity 6

Ask the children to name the fractions shaded on the shapes in Photocopiable Sheet Q.

Activity 7

Use Smarties and Smartie Fractions Sheets 1 and 2 (Photocopiable Sheets R and S) to reinforce the concept of fractions. This activity was invented by a colleague.

RESOURCES

- Biscuits
- Jug of water
- Two beakers
- Multilink
- Squared paper
- Coloured pencils
- Tubes of Smarties
- Smartie Fraction Sheets 1 and 2 (Photocopiable Sheets Q and R)

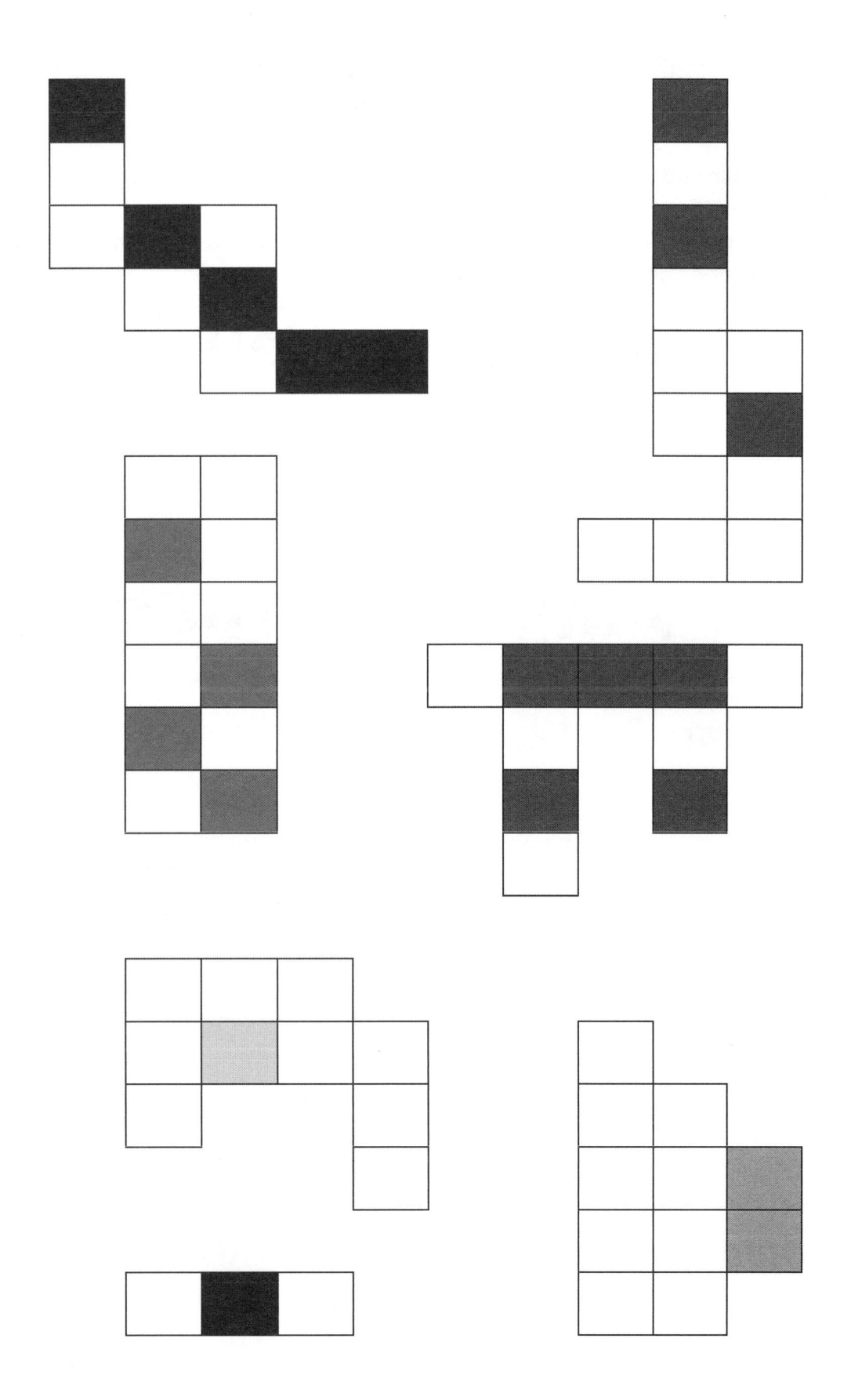

Photocopiable Sheet Q

Sheet 1

SMARTIE FRACTIONS

- Open your tube of Smarties and empty all the Smarties out.
- How many Smarties are there altogether?
- Separate the Smarties by colour into the sets on this page and write the total number of each colour inside the set.

Yellow

Blue

Pink

Green

Purple

Red

Brown

Orange

Photocopiable Sheet R

Sheet 2

SMARTIE FRACTIONS

- The total number of Smarties in a tube is the DENOMINATOR. The number of Smarties of a particular colour is the NUMERATOR.

    N: Number of a particular colour
    D: Total number of Smarties

- Using the information you have found out on Smarties Fractions Sheet 1, complete the following table.

Colour of Smartie	Number in a box	Fraction in a box	Equivalent fraction (if possible) e.g. 1/4

Photocopiable Sheet S

20 Negative Numbers

This is a difficult concept for many children to acquire. We mostly approach it through the reading of temperatures, where we can talk of being more or less than zero. However, there is the important concept of 'owing' that needs to be tackled by negative numbers.

As with other aspects of maths, working with money helps children grasp the meaning of negative numbers. We can illustrate this by examples such as:

Ben has £2 and he owes you £4. He gives you his £2, so how much does he owe now? He owes you £2, so he does not just have no money, he has a debt of £2. If Sally then gives him the £5 she owes him, what will happen? Of course, he will give you the £2 he owes you and then have £3.

This can all be expressed by £2 − £4 = −£2.   −£2 + £5 = £3.

A discussion of order in adding and subtracting should follow. Does it matter in what order we write the addition and subtraction in those two number sentences above?

While teaching a Year 6 group of children I was struck by how much more they needed to understand about negative numbers, and the sorts of problems they could be asked to solve with larger quantities, and how difficult they found it to grasp the concept of negativity. After a lot of experimentation on my computer I came up with the 200 oblong, shown as Photocopiable Sheet T. In making this oblong, I found that the only way it worked was to start with a 100 square with 0 in the bottom left-hand corner and with 99 at the top right-hand corner. This is a different way from that which is normally used, but now seems a very logical way of arranging 0 to 99, i.e., with the numbers getting larger as they rise. Conversely, counting back we get to 0 and then to −1, −2, and so on.

This oblong gives teacher and pupils ample opportunity to explore positive and negative numbers. Look at the oblong and then see examples of how it can be used in the following activity.

90	91	92	93	94	95	96	97	98	99
80	81	82	83	84	85	86	87	88	89
70	71	72	73	74	75	76	77	78	79
60	61	62	63	64	65	66	67	68	69
50	51	52	53	54	55	56	57	58	59
40	41	42	43	44	45	46	47	48	49
30	31	32	33	34	35	36	37	38	39
20	21	22	23	24	25	26	27	28	29
10	11	12	13	14	15	16	17	18	19
0	1	2	3	4	5	6	7	8	9
-10	-9	-8	-7	-6	-5	-4	-3	-2	-1
-20	-19	-18	-17	-16	-15	-14	-13	-12	-11
-30	-29	-28	-27	-26	-25	-24	-23	-22	-21
-40	-39	-38	-37	-36	-35	-34	-33	-32	-31
-50	-49	-48	-47	-46	-45	-44	-43	-42	-41
-60	-59	-58	-57	-56	-55	-54	-53	-52	-51
-70	-69	-68	-67	-66	-65	-64	-63	-62	-61
-80	-79	-78	-77	-76	-75	-74	-73	-72	-71
-90	-89	-88	-87	-86	-85	-84	-83	-82	-81
-100	-99	-98	-97	-96	-95	-94	-93	-92	-91

Photocopiable Sheet T

Activity

▶ Look at the oblong. What do you notice about the rows?

▶ What do you notice about the columns?

▶ Put your finger on 44 and take away 60 by going back in 10s. What number do you end on?

▶ What do you notice about the second digit in the number you started on and the number you ended on? (Note to teachers: 4 + 6 = 10. The same thing happens every time you take away 10s and end on a negative number.)

RESOURCES

- 200 oblong (Photocopiable Sheet T)
- OHP pens

21 What is the Bank Balance?

These questions will help pupils and teachers explore the 200 oblong and build mental images.

1. Conor has £12 in the bank. He gives Tesco a cheque for £22. How much will his overdraft be?

2. Chris has a balance of £44. She owes Alican £50. How much more money will she need before she can pay him?

3. On Tuesday Alex discovers that she has an overdraft of £21. She then pays in a cheque for £40. How much will her balance be now?

4. Andy pays £30 for a new computer game. He pays with his credit card. However he only has £11 in the bank. What will his overdraft be?

5. You have £33 in the bank and your uncle pays in another £42 for you. You then buy some designer jeans for £100. What will your bank balance be?

6. Oh dear! Your overdraft is £220. You open a letter and are happy to find that you have a cheque for £200 from your aunt. What is the state of your bank balance after you pay this in?

7. Jenny needs £65 to pay her bill from Peter Jones. She only has £26. How much more does she need?

8. After Ben paid a bill for £75 he had an overdraft of £15. How much did he have in the bank to begin with?

9. Louis has £459.01. He gives his best friend a cheque for £683.92. What will his balance be now?

10. If you have £50 in the bank and this increases by 5% each six months, how much will you have at the end of 5 years?

22 Mental Arithmetic

To be an efficient mathematician, it is important to develop mental arithmetic skills. Many children have difficulties remembering facts and using them. For the child with mathematical difficulties the temptation is to restrict the curriculum. Thus, many children continue to use concrete materials, with little time spent on developing mental arithmetic.

In Fairley House, we decided that a good use of our weekly junior assembly was to practise counting and counting sequences while having fun. The following are some of the activities that the children enjoy – and they do help!

Activity 1

Use a pendulum and ask children to count to the beat of the pendulum. Start with counting in 1s, in 2s, in 5s and in 10s. The children then count on and back. As our audience comprises children from ages 6 to 11, it is important to keep the interest of all. The speed can be varied. Children can be specially chosen to count according to their ability. The more able can be asked to count on and back in 5s starting from 1, 2, 3 or 4. Do not forget that counting in 100s, 1,000s and 1,000,000s gives lovely big numbers and a sense of achievement for most children.

Activity 2

Use a counting stick (Figure 22.1) to practise the activities in Activity 1. Do not always start at 0. You can start anywhere on the stick. If counting in 5s the middle number is 25.

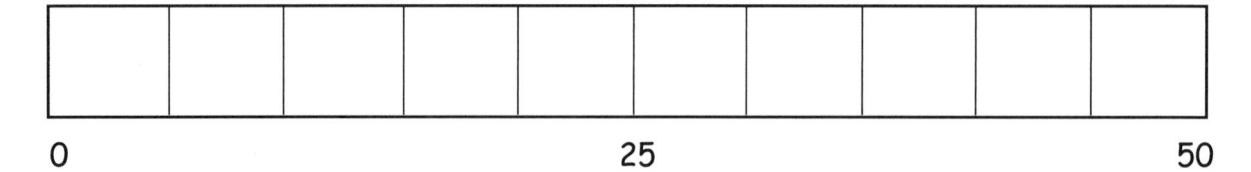

0   25   50

Figure 22.1: A counting stick

Continue this theme with other counting sequences.

Activity 3

Introduce fractions of numbers. Which number is half-way along the stick? Choose the sequences with care. Half-way in any sequence can be found fairly easily. Only the most able child could say what number is quarter of the way along the stick. Younger or less able children are experiencing more number language than they would normally get in their maths group.

Activity 4

Choose children to use the pendulum and the number stick. They tend to be keen to show their knowledge, and by giving them a free choice of sequences, they do not feel threatened.

Activity 5

Introduce exercise into the counting. Start with the children sitting on the floor. Ask them to count in 2s, starting at 0 and following the exercise sequence of two hands on the head and then on the shoulder, head, shoulder. Repeat with other counting sequences.

Activity 6

Vary the exercises by varying the number of moves, e.g. touch head, shoulders and chest, head, shoulders, chest.

Activity 7

Children stand up and follow a counting and exercise sequence. You can be very inventive with this – the more movement the better!

All this leads very naturally to chanting tables, both multiplication and division tables.

Children can lead any of the above activities. One or more can decide on an exercise and counting sequence and lead it. Children become ever more inventive. We have found that the children's understanding, remembering and use of number sequences improve as we continue to retain this vital part of mathematics as part of our assembly.

RESOURCES

- Pendulum
- Counting stick

23 Mental Arithmetic Using Number Cards

Many children find it difficult to learn number bonds to 10, to 20, to 50, to 100. We can chant them in class. We can write them down. We can discuss them and find patterns. We can also make it fun by playing a game and having a competition. I find that number cards can be used in lots of games; each time we play one game, another suggests itself.

NUMBER CARD GAMES

Activity 1

Make sets of number cards each showing a single number, 0 to 10, 11 to 20 etc. (as high as you want to go). These can be used with children of all ages. For the least able, or those practising early number skills, choose the number cards 0 to 10. Place cards face up on the table or floor. The teacher asks each child to find two cards that total a number (e.g. 15).

Activity 2

I find that playing in teams galvanises children to use all sorts of strategies to win a point. You should divide the class into teams. You should choose a child from each team (carefully matching ability) and ask them to stand up. The following instructions could be given:

'Find two cards that total 42.'
'Find three cards that total 34.'
'Find two cards with a difference of 13.'
'Find two cards that, when multiplied together, give a total of 36.'
'Find two cards so that one can be divided into the other and give an answer of 7.'
'Find two cards, so that one is half (double) the other.'
'Find two cards, so that one is a quarter of the other.'

There are endless possibilities.

The first child to find the correct cards gains a point for his or her team. You can choose the level of difficulty by deciding which cards to use. Rules can be made up or changed. It will be found necessary, for many games, to remove the 0.

RESOURCES

- Sets of laminated number cards: 0 to 10, 11 to 20, 21 to 30, 31 to 40, 41 to 50, 51 to 60, 61 to 70, 71 to 80, 81 to 90, 91 to 100. You may decide to use numbers up to 50 only. These will give plenty of scope for games.

24 Activities Using Dice

Dice are cheap to buy, easy to use, and lend themselves to a variety of activities. The following are some ideas that we have found useful. They can also be given to parents as suggestions of ways in which they can help their children at home. This emphasises to parents that children do not need to be filling in worksheets to be learning maths. As they begin to use dice more, pupils, teachers and parents should find it easy to invent their own games.

▶ Activity 1

Use two dice numbered 1 to 6. Players take it in turn to throw dice and add the numbers shown. The one with the highest total wins a point. Do this until one player has gained ten points; he or she is the winner.

▶ Activity 2

Play the same game as in Activity 1, but this time the person whose dice have the lowest total wins a point.

▶ Activity 3

Use three dice to play the above two games.

▶ Activity 4

Use two dice. Players take it in turn to throw dice and take one number from the other. The person with the highest total wins a point. The player who first gains ten points is the winner.

▶ Activity 5

Play the same game as in Activity 4, but with the lowest total winning a point.

Activity 6

Throw two dice numbered 1 to 6. Multiply one number by the other. Work out the answer using counters, a 100 square, or pictures. Make up your own rules to find a winner.

Activity 7

This is a game for up to four players and practises addition and place value. Each player has a laminated card (Photocopiable Sheet U). Players take it in turn to throw two dice and add the totals. They record their scores by tallying in the 1s column. When they have ten in the column they rub this out and put a one in the 10s column. Each player has, say, five goes. The winner is the one with the highest total.

Activity 8

Repeat the above game, using variations as in the other games above (subtraction, multiplication).

Activity 9

Practise mutiplication. Use blank dice and put on them the numbers in the table you want to practise. For example, if you want to practise multiplying by two you could number your two dice: a) 0, 1, 2, 3, 4, 5 and b) 0, 6, 7, 8, 9, 10. Play first with the die numbered 0 to 5. Each player takes it in turn to throw the die and multiplies the number shown by two, noting his or her score. The first to reach, say, 30 is the winner. Now repeat the game using the other die, and increase the winning total.

RESOURCES

- For each pair of players, two dice numbered 1 to 6 and a pair of blank dice
- Counters, 100 square or pictures
- Laminated board (Photocopiable Sheet U)
- OHP pens

10s	1s

Photocopiable Sheet U

25 Practising Basic Number Skills with Monster Maths

There comes a time when children have to learn to use the written number system, to read sums and to work out the answers. It is often at this stage that the child becomes confused by the procedures to which he or she has been introduced. In order for learning not to become automated and thus fail in a problem-solving situation, it must be presented in a variety of ways. This is where we can have fun.

Here is how Monster Maths works. The children are given a series of number problems to work out. The answer to each one gives them the number of bodies, heads, eyes, ears and so on of the monster. The children then draw the monster.

Here are some examples of monsters, but be inventive!

Monster 1:

bodies:	$100 \div 100$	heads:	$(4 + 6) \div 2$
eyes:	$(2 \times 4) + (3 \times 5)$	noses:	$2 \times (18 \div 9)$
mouths:	$(50 \div 10) \times 2$	ears:	$(25 + 5) \div 2$
arms:	$1/4$ of 40	fingers:	$1/2$ of 40
legs:	$(30 + 6) \div 9$	feet:	$1/3$ of 12

Photocopiable Sheet V sets out the instructions for this monster and Figures 25.1 and 25.2 are monsters made to these instructions by children in my class.

Monster 2:

bodies:	$50 - 49$	heads:	$12 - 3$
eyes:	$(2 \times 4) + 4$	noses:	$16 - 2$
mouths:	4×4	ears:	$8 - 2$
arms:	4×6	fingers:	24×2
legs:	2×7	feet:	7×2

Decorate body with two triangles, three quadrilaterals and a hexagon.

Monster 3:

bodies:	50% of 2	heads:	$1/4$ of 12
eyes:	$2/3$ of 6	noses:	20% of 40
mouths:	$3/5$ of 10	ears:	10% of 40
arms:	$3/4$ of 12	fingers:	$3/4$ of 24
legs:	15% of 40, with double that number of feet		

64 *Number*

RESOURCES

- A set of instructions (e.g. Photocopiable Sheet V)
- Paper
- Pencils
- Coloured pencils
- Felt tips
- Concrete objects for calculating
- Calculator if using certain skills
- Scraps of paper or pieces of wool, etc. if you decide to decorate your monsters

Maths Monster

Draw a Maths Monster by following these instructions:

bodies:	$100 \div 100$
heads:	$(4 + 6) \div 2$
eyes:	$(2 \times 4) + (3 \times 5)$
noses:	$2 \times (18 \div 9)$
mouths:	$(50 \div 10) \times 2$
ears:	$(25 + 5) \div 2$
arms:	$\frac{1}{4}$ of 40
fingers:	$\frac{1}{2}$ of 40
legs:	$(30 + 6) \div 9$
feet:	$\frac{1}{3}$ of 12

Figure 25.1: Maths monster 1

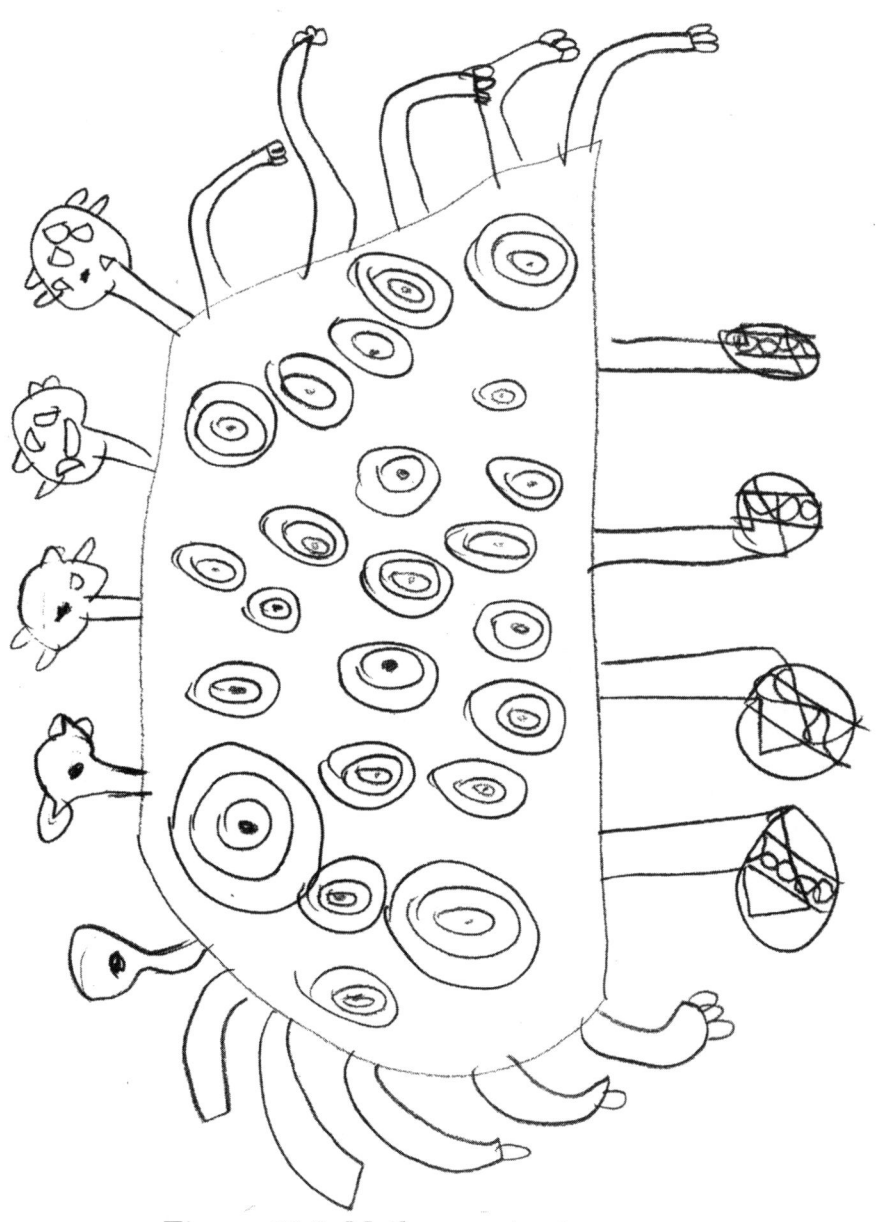

Practising Basic Number Skills with Monster Maths 67

bodies	1
heads	5
noses	4
mouths	10
eyes	23
arms	10
fingers	20
ears	15
legs	4
feet	4

Figure 25.2: Maths monster 1

26 Blockbusters

This is a game that a colleague introduced to our maths group. The children loved playing it and it really made them think. I shall give you some ideas of how we used the game. You can, no doubt, make up many more.

You will need a honeycomb made up of hexagons (see Photocopiable Sheet W). Each child needs a photocopy. You could also laminate enough for the class so that they can be used over and over. I find putting them on an overhead transparency and using them with an OHP can save a lot of time and gives a very flexible resource. Here is how you can play Blockbusters with your class.

Divide the children into two teams. The object of the game is to cross the honeycomb from west to east or north to south, moving horizontally, vertically or diagonally. The children take it in turn to answer a question, choosing the hexagon they want to tackle. Hexagons are won by giving a correct answer. If the wrong answer is given the other team is given a free turn, but must answer the same question. They then take their own turn in the normal way. The first team to go from one side of the honeycomb to the other is the winner.

Lots of procedures and facts can be rehearsed and used in this game.

▶ Activity 1

Write addition and subtraction sums (of a suitable challenge – this depending on the children you teach) in the hexagons.

▶ Activity 2

Write multiplication questions in the hexagons.

▶ Activity 3

Write division questions in hexagons.

Activity 4

The children can practise algebra by the teacher leaving one figure out of each sum, e.g.

10 – ☐ = 4   15 = ☐ – 5

Activity 5

Use problems that miss out the mathematical sign, e.g.

10 ☐ 5 = 2   10 ☐ 5 = 50

Activity 6

Use the same types of problems as above, but in a different way. Put some 'answers' in the hexagons and ask the children to give suitable questions.

Activity 7

Write numbers (using digits) in the hexagons and the children have to write the *words* underneath.

Activity 8

Use a variety of the above.

This game is also useful for developing planning strategies as the children should try to block each other. The teacher could also throw in a mystery hexagon, which could be marked with a large **?**

which could be any question to do with the maths facts that the children are currently learning, e.g. 'What is the seventh month of the year?'

RESOURCES

- Hexagon grid on OHP (Photocopiable Sheet W)
- Laminated hexagon grids for each child
- OHP pens
- Set of questions

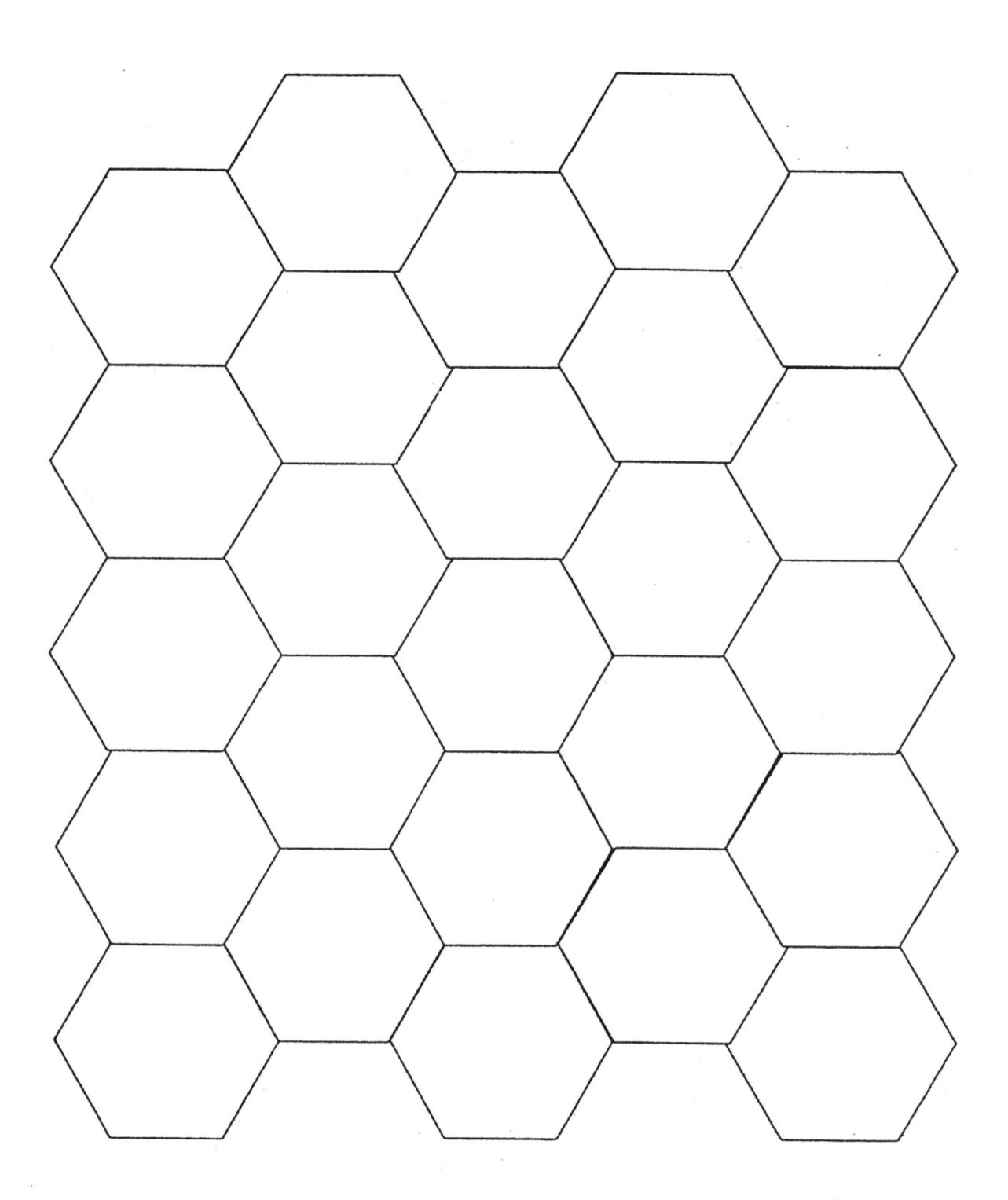

Photocopiable Sheet W

27   A Project on Travel

A colleague decided to use the Internet to explore practical ways of extending work previously done in maths lessons. The following pages outline some of the activities he did with his maths group. They grabbed the interest of this group of pupils, who did not find maths easy.

The following are suggested activities for teachers. They lend themselves to expansion and adaptation.

▶ Activity 1: Explore the time and cost of travel

Ask the pupils to decide on a range of possible holiday destinations and the dates they want to travel. Use the Internet to access relevant sites that will give details of travel routes, times and costs. (The following are useful and easy to use: British Airways, Easyjet, Eurostar.)

Ask the pupils the following questions:

1. What date and time do you want to travel and what time is this using the 24-hour clock?
2. How many companies have transport leaving at that time? Have a look at the costs on various days. Are some days cheaper to travel on than others? If so, why?
3. What time would you arrive at your destination on various different days? (This may entail looking at time differences across zones.)
4. How long do various flights take to get you to your destination? Rank responses in order of time taken, shortest to longest.
5. How much does each company charge? Rank your means of transport in order of cost, lowest to highest.
6. What connection is there, if any, between the answers to questions 4 and 5?

▶ Activity 2: Explore the cost of accommodation

Choose one destination. Pupils need to be able to access a variety of sites. You can decide to limit these according to the intended outcome of the lesson. Pupils could look at hotel or villa accommodation, or both. It is easier, initially, to choose just one type of accommodation.

In this activity you need to decide on which websites to use. You could choose a particular hotel chain to access. You could find a tourist information office at each of the destinations. Questions posed to pupils will depend on what access they have. You should give pupils a destination each. These are possible questions:

1. What is the difference in price between the cheapest and dearest hotel at your destination?
2. Can you find the average price for a 2-star, 3-star, 4-star and 5-star hotel?
3. You have a budget of £x to spend on accommodation for a week. Which hotel would you choose? (Look at what is included in the cost.)
4. What is the cost in local currency and sterling? (You could use a currency converter or find out 'the hard way'.)
5. How much would it be for a family of two adults and two children?
6. If you add on the cost of travel, how much does the holiday cost?
7. Which destination is the cheapest, and which the dearest?
8. If you rented a villa instead, what would be the difference in cost?
9. What would make you choose one type of accommodation over another?

Activity 3: Eating on holiday

Teachers can be creative here. You could find menus from certain hotels. You can write lists of local food and decide on appropriate prices. Information can be gained from the Internet, but you can come up with your own worksheets. You should remember to use the local currency when quoting prices.

Pupils answer the following questions.

1. About how much would a meal cost in Hotel x? Convert this to sterling.
2. Compare this with the price of a meal in two other hotels, one cheaper and one more expensive. What is the difference in price between the meals?
3. If you and your family were to have a picnic, what would you buy and how much would you spend?
4. How much would it cost to cook a meal for yourselves?
5. Look at the prices of products at your destination and in Britain. Which products are dearer here and which are cheaper? (Pupils will need to convert currency.)
6. If you had £x to spend on food over the week, how would you spend it?

By this stage of the topic, pupils should be getting a lot more insight into the costs of holidays and the choices to be made. This topic could take any length of time, depending on organisation and how much depth teachers want to go into. It links well with other aspects of the curriculum, e.g. science and geography.

Activity 4: What about the weather?

This gives pupils a chance to think about weather in other parts of the world and what effect weather has on our holidays and choice of destination. For instance, when choosing a beach holiday people want sun and warmth. When going skiing they want something rather different!

You should collect information about the holiday destination over one week. This can be done from a newspaper, or through a website. Each pupil should be allocated a destination and then asked the following questions:

1. What was the average temperature over the week?
2. On how many days did it rain?
3. Which days were warm but cloudy?
4. (For those looking at a ski resort.) Was there sufficient snow each day?

Various websites (e.g. BBC Weather) could be used to study graphs of weather conditions. These allow the following questions to be posed:

1. In which month is the average temperature lowest/highest?
2. In which month is the average rainfall lowest/highest?
3. Which months had the lowest/highest average hours of sunshine?

Finally, round off the project by discussing all the issues raised. What makes some holiday destinations more or less attractive for different people? Think about how many people have a choice of holiday destinations and about all those who do not.

As you can see, this project lends itself to expansion into many areas of the curriculum. There are endless possibilities. Pupils can be involved in organising field trips. They can use a day trip as a project.

RESOURCES

- Pencils
- Paper
- The Internet

28 Who Wants to be a Maths Millionaire?

This game was adapted by a colleague at Fairley House. It is played according to the rules of the well-known television game. I am putting it into this section on numeracy, but it can be altered to suit work on all areas of the maths curriculum.

The children in the class are the audience. The challenger sits in a chair opposite the teacher who has a list of questions and the challenger can gain money in the same way as happens in the television game. One correct answer gives the challenger £100, a second doubles this to £200 and so on. The top prize is, of course, £1,000,000. You can produce cheques made out with the set amounts.

The same lifelines are available as are seen the show; the challenger can phone a friend, go 50/50 or ask the audience. Questions can be targeted at the specific child and be used to revise recent work, to revise past work or to challenge.

This game ensures that all the children in the class become involved in the quiz and are eager to find the answers themselves, even when they are not the challenger. My colleague has found this a very successful way to involve the whole class in an enjoyable game in which a lot of learning takes place.

The following questions can be used for this game. Pick the set that best suits your class or group. For each question asked you need to supply four possible answers of which only one is correct.

Questions Set 1

1. Add together 33 and 27.
2. Two numbers together total 79. If one number is 36, what is the other?
3. What is 18 minus 9?
4. If four times a number is 16, what is that number?
5. Add 12, 13 and 27 and find half of the total.
6. Multiply 13 by 2.
7. Add £1.30, 70p and £1.40.
8. What is one-half as a percentage?
9. What number comes next? 3, 6, 10, 15,
10. How many weeks in 42 days?
11. How long would it take to save £10 if you saved 50p each week?
12. If a packet of tea cost £1.25, how much are three packets?
13. What is one-sixth of 60?

14. A rectangle has an area of 15 square centimetres. It is 5cm wide. How long is it?
15. What is another way of saying 1.45 p.m.?

Questions Set 2

1. Add together 31, 69, 50 and 27.
2. What is 48 divided by 8?
3. What is the value of 3 squared?
4. A currant bun costs 24p. How much do six cost?
5. How many weeks in 77 days?
6. What is 6.45 p.m. on the 24-hour clock?
7. You paid £45 for a shirt and some gloves. The gloves cost £1.75. How much was the shirt?
8. Multiply 1.4 by 10.
9. If 45g of cheese cost 90p, how much do 65g cost?
10. A newspaper cost 55p a day from Monday to Friday. How much do you spend during this time?
11. What is the average of 2, 4 and 6?
12. Write these in order, smallest first: 2, 5.8, 0.6, 8.5, 6
13. Divide 3,570 by 10.
14. If a room measures 10.25 metres by 2.45 metres, what is the perimeter?
15. There are 360 seats in a small cinema. There are 45 seats in each row. How many rows are there?

Questions Set 3

1. How many hours between 8.30 a.m. and 9.30 p.m.?
2. How many cm in 3m?
3. How many days in January and February in a leap year?
4. If one side of a rectangle measures 7.5cm and another measures 5.5cm, what is the perimeter of the rectangle?
5. How may millilitres in half a litre?
6. How would you write 20 minutes to seven in the evening, using the 24-hour clock?
7. How many years, months and days from 25 June 1991 to 4 July 1995?
8. Tom weighs 15.5 kilos at birth. He puts on 10%. What does he weigh now?
9. A group of children weigh 24kg, 26kg, 22kg, 21kg and 27kg. What is their average weight?
10. How many millilitres in 26.5 centilitres?
11. I go to bed at 22.00. I read for 45 minutes. I wake at 06.15. How long do I sleep?
12. Jack jogged, on average, 5.25km an hour. How far did he jog in two and a half hours?
13. If you bought half a kilo of potatoes at 74p a kilo, butter for £1.05 and two dozen eggs at 85p per dozen, how much change would you get from £10?

76 *Number*

14. If a euro is worth 66 pence, how many euros would you get for £6.93?
15. How many minutes in 3.75 hours?

RESOURCES

- Sets of questions with possible answers
- A laminated graph (for 'Ask the audience')
- Paper and Blu-Tack to cover up questions (for '50/50')
- Cheques

29 Multiplication Tables

Many children find it difficult to remember multiplication tables. Children with mathematical learning difficulties may find it almost impossible to remember a large number of facts and to readily recall them to help solve a problem. Constant repetition helps, but children need to accept that they may not always be able to recall at will. They must be encouraged to think through the meaning of their work and be willing to work out answers. This may seem an obvious comment to make, but there is still an overemphasis, in some quarters, on the need to learn multiplication by heart. It is important that children have the practical experience necessary to really understand the concept. Such experience also helps children to build up mental images to which they can refer when needed.

We have found that a large number of children coming to our school, be they in Year 3 or Year 5, have not had the experience necessary to give them an understanding of the concepts of multiplication and division. To them 'tables' are lists of meaningless facts. We often have to work hard to help them build up their own understanding and to give them the confidence to think things through. Many of the children have limited understanding of sequences and number patterns.

I have found it useful to introduce maths into the weekly assembly with the younger children in the school (aged 6 to 9). We have fun using a counting stick, a pendulum apple and exercises to practise counting sequences. Here are some of the activities from our assembly.

▶ Activity 1

Ask the children to count in steps of 1, 2, etc., keeping time with the pendulum apple. You can vary the speed according to the ability of the children and the sequence being practised. Counting in 2s is easy for most children.

▶ Activity 2

Choose various groups of children to count, according to ability, so that you can match challenge to children.

78   Number

Activity 3

Use a counting stick, with ten steps. The children count as you touch each division of the stick. Start at 0 and count in 2s, 4s, etc. Emphasise the mid-point. Count forwards and backwards.

Activity 4

Start at numbers other than 0, e.g. count forwards and backwards in 3s, 4s, etc., starting from 1.

Activity 5

Introduce exercise into the session. Choose two movements to begin with. For instance you can demonstrate counting in 2, touching your head then your shoulders while counting. The sequence can be varied as well as the type and number of movements.

Activity 6

Ask children to volunteer to make up a movement sequence and suggest a counting sequence to accompany it. For instance, counting in 2s the child leading the counting uses two hands to touch their head, shoulders, chest and knees, counting 0, 2, 4, 6. They go back to the beginning of their movement sequence to continue 8, 10, 12, 14, and so it goes on. Children can be very inventive. It is a good idea to keep the movements few and simple to begin with.

Activity 7

Build up tables with Multilink or other concrete material (see Figure 29.1). Use this opportunity to build up the children's understanding of maths language, varying language as much as possible (lots of, groups of, sets of, boxes of). Ask the children to make up multiplication sentences using the language. Then build up the tables using squared paper, writing the number of squares at the end of each line.

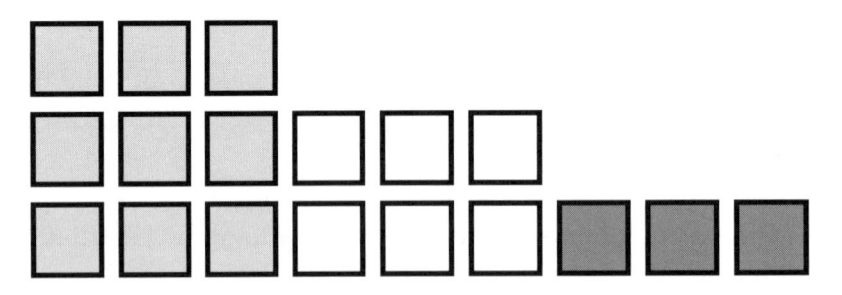

Figure 29.1: 3 times table using Multilink

Activity 8

Build up the 2 times table using 2p coins (calculating the total every time you add another coin). Do the same with 5p coins, and then with 10p coins (Figure 29.2).

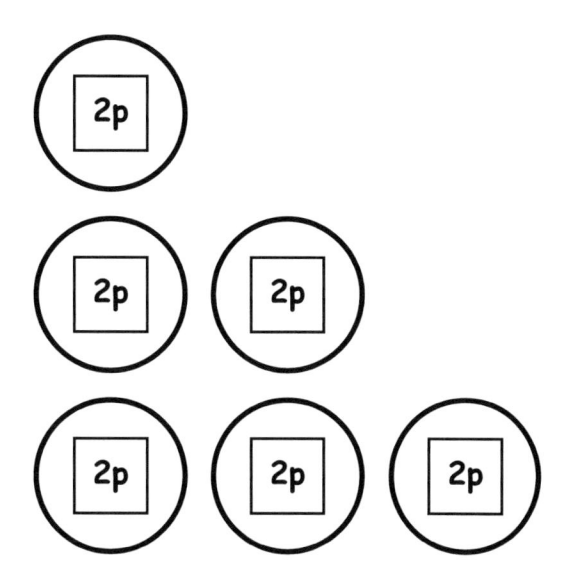

Figure 29.2

Activity 9

Work out multiplication with pictures. Give the children a picture of boxes, each containing two objects. How many are there in one box? How many are there altogether in two boxes? Make up other pictures to practise other multiplication series.

Activity 10

Use a laminated 100 square to colour in multiplication patterns. Use three sheets to colour in a) the pattern of 2, b) the pattern of 4, c) the pattern of 8. Children will see that once they know one fact they often know several others. The discussion in this type of exercise helps children to understand patterns and sequences and their relationship to multiplication (see Photocopiable Sheet X).

Activity 11

Again, this is an opportunity to show children that once they know one fact they often know several others. Use spot patterns to relate the four rules of number:

● ● ● ● $2 + 2 + 2 + 2 = 8$

● ● ● ● $8 - 2 - 2 - 2 - 2 = 0$

4 lots of 2 make 8 ($4 \times 2 = 8$)

2 lots of 4 make 8 ($2 \times 4 = 8$)

How many 2s in 8?

How many 4s in 8?

Activity 12

Once the children have had all this practical experience they can make their own multiplication square (see Photocopiable Sheet W).

RESOURCES

- Pendulum
- Counting stick
- Multilink
- Plastic coins (2p, 5p, 10p)
- Squared paper
- Picture of boxes each containing two objects
- Laminated 100 square (Photocopiable Sheet X)

Multiplication Square

×	0	1	2	3	4	5	6	7	8	9	10
0											
1											
2											
3											
4											
5											
6											
7											
8											
9											
10											

Photocopiable Sheet X

30 Finger Tables

Despite all your hard work, the children still do not remember their tables! Teach them finger tables. I first saw these in action when I visited Fairley House in 1989. When you have tried them, visualise my walking into a room and seeing ten children manipulating their fingers in strange ways!

They have been the subject of an article in the *Times Educational Supplement* and Anne Henderson describes their use in her book *Maths and Dyslexics* (St David's College, Llandudno 1989, ISBN: 0 9512529 17). Figure 30.1 shows how I prefer to number fingers to work out 6 to 10 times tables. It is assumed that children know 2 to 5 times tables. The 10 times table would be known to almost all children.

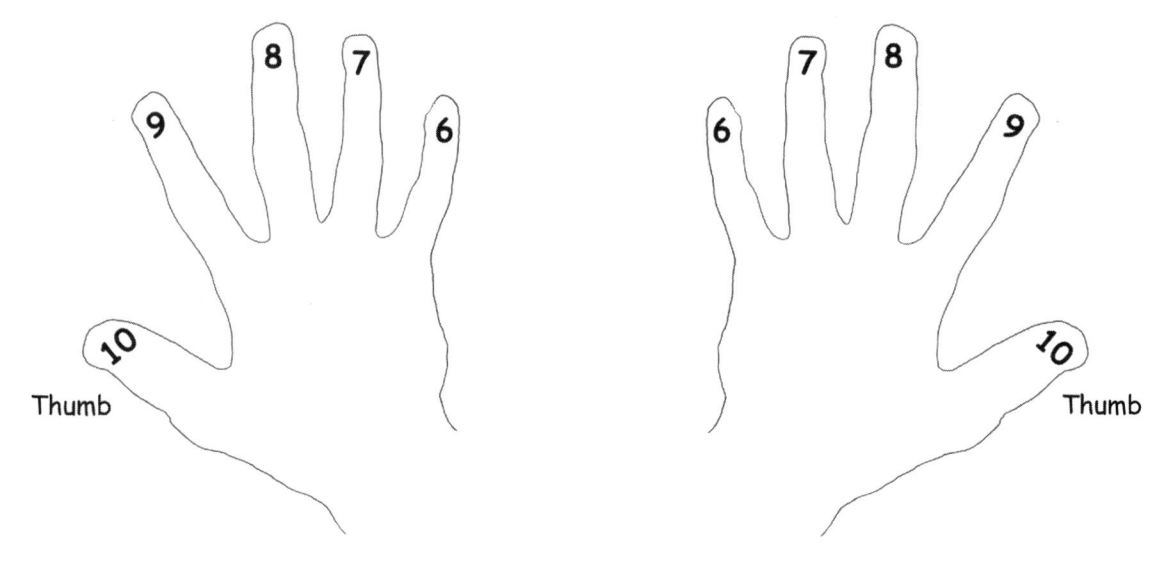

Figure 30.1: How to mark fingers for finger tables

Instructions to children

- Hold your hands palm up in front of you. Write the numbers 6 to 10 in felt tips on your fingers as shown in Figure 30.1.
- To find 6 × 8, take the 6 fingertip of one hand and place it against the 8 fingertip of the other hand. The two fingers touching (2) and the two furthest away from the body (2) are the tens, i.e. 2 + 2 = 4; four 10s make 40.
- The fingers left number four on one hand and two on the other. Multiply 4 by 2 and this gives you 8.
- You now have 40 and 8, which makes 48.

Finger Tables 83

Now try this with other numbers, e.g. 7 × 7 or 9 × 8. As you can see, it can be used for the 9 times table, but the next figure (30.2) is the easiest and most efficient.

Multiplying by 9 is easy. First of all look at the patterns.

$$1 \times 9 = 9$$
$$2 \times 9 = 18$$
$$3 \times 9 = 27$$

If you continue this sequence you will notice two things:

- The sum of the digits in the 'answers' comes to 9.
- If you are multiplying 9 by another number, e.g. 8; the answer will begin with the digit before this in our counting sequence, e.g. 7. The second digit in the answer can be added to the first to make 9, in this case the number will be 2. 9 × 8 = 72.

You can use this different finger table for the 9 times table as follows (again, see the above references).

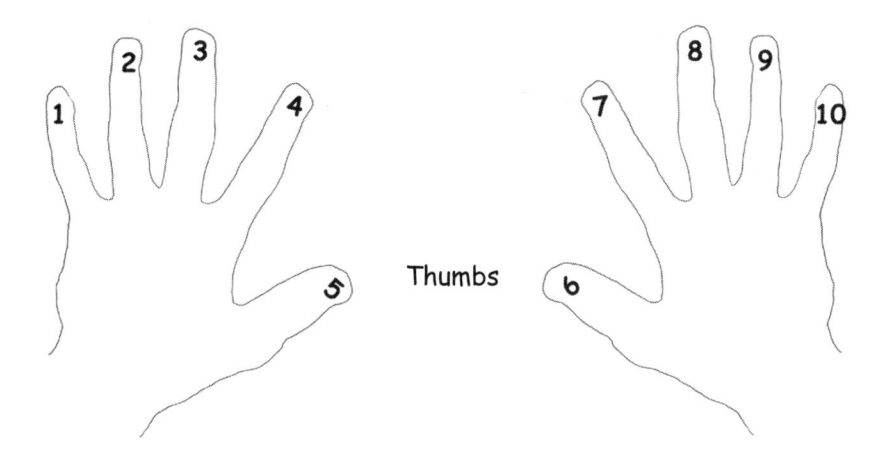

Figure 30.2: How to mark fingers for the 9 times table

Instructions to children

- Place your hands face down on the table, (I prefer this way of using the hands and fingers as it is easier for the children to keep the fingers in place.)
- Number your nails 1 to 10 as shown in Figure 30.2.
- To find 1 × 9, curl back the number 1 finger. The fingers to the right are the 1s, so the answer is 9.
- To find 3 × 9, curl back the number 3 finger. The fingers to the left of this are the 10s, i.e. two 10s or 20. The fingers to the right are the 1s, i.e. seven 1s or 7. The answer is 27.

The above exercises have helped lots of children, but should not be taught at the expense of understanding. At each step, make sure that the children understand what multiplication is (and division). The finger tables do take the drudgery and fear out of some situations, especially timed tests and exams.

31 Three in a Row – a Tables Game

This is an activity that we were introduced to by a visiting American teacher some years ago. It is intended to help children learn their multiplication tables, and be willing to work out answers that do not come readily to mind. It has been used successfully ever since.

Activity 1

Construct a grid as illustrated in Figure 31.1 and number the ends of the line as shown.

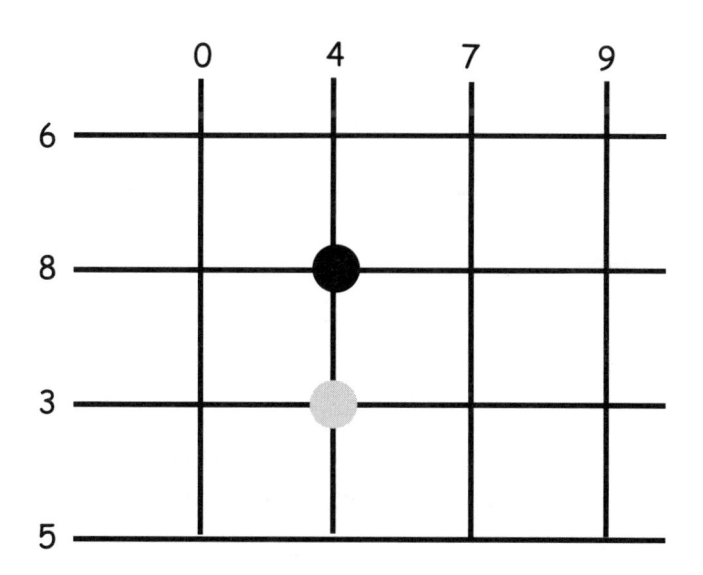

Figure 31.1: Example of grid used for revising tables

Teachers can choose any numbers, depending on what multiplication tables they want the children to revise.

▶ Divide children into two teams. Each team takes it in turn to multiply two numbers together and give the answer. For instance, team A could choose 8 × 4 is 32. The teacher would mark the intersection with a coloured blob, for example, red. The object of the game is to get three answers in a row, be it diagonal, horizontal or vertical.

86 Number

▶ Team B will try to block team A, and vice versa. In the above, team B might choose 3 × 4 is 12 and the teacher could mark this with a blue blob. The game continues until one team has won. Prizes can be given.

Activity 2

▶ Practise addition and subtraction facts by playing 'Three in a row' using numbers appropriate to the age and ability of the children you are teaching. Figure 31.2 shows a game where children are practising adding two two-digit numbers mentally.

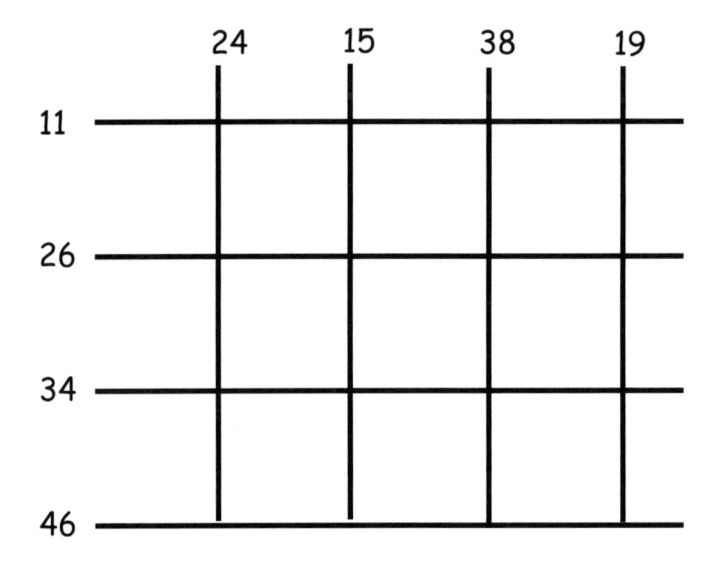

Figure 31.2: Example of grid used for mental addition of two-digit numbers

Activity 3

▶ A more sophisticated version could involve adding fractions.
▶ What about finding a fraction or percentage of a number? Be inventive!

RESOURCES

- An appropriate grid (e.g. Figure 31.1)
- Coloured pens